RECOVERING HIS I

This remarkable book on leading a chu
many decades of proclaiming Christ
Overflowing with honesty, wisdom and insight, it should be compulsory reading for all who are called to be shepherds of God's flock. Recommended without reservation!
J. John – author and International Evangelist.

This account of a remarkable ministry is noteworthy not only for the autobiographical content but the honesty with which both failure and success are recounted. This is a valuable guide not only as to how to organise the life of a growing congregation but also how to keep fresh the vision and vocation which inspired Stuart to ministry in the first place. As one who served alongside Stuart in this diocese — we were ordained in the same year— his account of ministry in rural West Wales resonates with my own, as does the learning curve over time and, hopefully, the wisdom which comes from experience, and enables them to be applied to a wider sphere of ministry.
+J. Wyn Evans – former Bishop of St Davids.

Stuart Bell is one of the best preachers of his generation. The roots of that ministry stem from the depth of his heart as a Minister Evangelist. This book captures the warmth of Stuart's love for Christ, His people and His church. It tells the inspiring story of God's work in Aberystwyth as well as offering wise insights and sharp challenges for the church today. It did much good to my soul.
+John Holbrook – Bishop of Brixworth.

'Recovering His Reputation' is a fascinating and instructive outline of the biblical principles behind Stuart Bell's ministry, with his wife Pru, over many years in West Wales. I have only recently come into personal contact with Stuart as he launched Fellowship 345 which, as he tells us proved to bear an uncanny resemblance to the 'accidental prophecy' in his interview with Llewellyn Jenkins in 2004. (For more on this, read the chapter entitled 'An accidental prophecy'). Stuart is absolutely right when he says that 'the

authority of the Bible is the underlying issue in why initiatives such as Fellowship 345 are necessary; this diagnosis leading to his prognosis for the future of the church in Wales suggest that we would do well to pay heed to the principles that undergirded his ministry, particularly at St Michael's Aberystwyth, as explained to us in this book.
+Andy Lines – Anglican Convocation in Europe.

I first met Stuart Bell when he spoke at Lampeter College in 1977. I was immediately struck by his passionate love for Jesus and his burning passion for people. From the colliding of those passions has grown one of the most successful leadership ministries in Wales of recent years. Together, Stuart and Pru have led successfully and consistently in evangelism, discipleship, and church growth, and the principles and fruit of that ministry are well documented in this book. Stuart's leadership skills were not learned from a book, taught in a classroom, or formulated at a desk, but worked out at the tough coal face of day-to-day church leadership. I know how hard that has sometimes been, and the sacrificial cost involved. To have shared alongside Stuart in a small part of the ministry in St Michael's remains one of the great privileges of my own ministry. So, I commend this book to all who are seeking to develop and hone their own leadership in the rapidly changing world and church of today.
Andy Herrick – Archdeacon of Anglesey.

I loved reading this book. Stuart's love for the Lord, his Church - and people everywhere shines out of each chapter and I've found myself stirred and challenged by it. It is full of practical wisdom that Stuart has derived directly from the Lord and through his deep knowledge of the Bible, and also through his openness to listen and learn from others - and hammered out on the anvil of his experience of many years of fruitful ministry. It is a great read for any Christian, but I especially commend it to anyone called to leadership of a Church or other Kingdom venture. I wish I had read it years ago!
Bruce Collins – New Wine Cymru Leadership Team

Those working with the Christian Research agency had an interesting time in interpreting their research practically for local churches. We had the privilege of doing this for many, including St Michael's in Aberystwyth, thus meeting (and staying) with Stuart Bell and his wife. The sessions seemed to go well but on the Sunday morning before going to church, Stuart asked me, "Let me know if there's anything in the service that you think could be improved," a task I'd never done before for a service. I gave him my observations afterwards, but his challenging request kept coming back, "How can we do better?" – something to ask in every situation. Thank you, Stuart, for your encouragement and help! That's what this book is all about.
Peter Brierley – Director of Brierley Consultants

I was expecting to enjoy Stuart Bell's account of ministry in St Michael's Aberystwyth - the church where I worshipped in my student years. But I did not expect an account so gripping and challenging in every chapter. A wonderful blend of honest personal narrative, biblical reflection, quiet meditation and detailed practical insights, it offers an invaluable resource for anyone at any stage in Christian ministry. The author's transparency, his readiness to point to mistakes and failures as well as share God's enormous blessings opens us all up to self-examination before God, and deepens our longing for integrity. My advice is to buy the book now. It could save a lot of grief later!
Elaine Storkey – Philosopher, Sociologist, Theologian

I sometimes wonder what I'd be like if I could combine the energy and drive I had when young with the wisdom I imagine I have acquired through experience. In this book, Stuart Bell shares wisdom he's learned from long years of notable church leadership to help others get wiser faster. This isn't just theory – Stuart distils his wisdom from the story of St Michael's Aberystwyth told in a very readable way. Hard-won wisdom about prayer, small groups, encouraging people, growth ceilings, staff teams, evangelism, decision making, conflict, preaching, self-care and the rest is shared with clarity and humility. One piece of Stuart's wisdom is 'don't copy other people' but we do learn from them – and there is plenty

for any church leader to learn from in this engaging story of Stuart and St Michael's growing together and recovering the reputation of Jesus in the town they served.
Bob Jackson – Archdeacon, author, church growth adviser

Reading 'Recovering His Reputation' is a bit like being on a fair ground roller coaster ride: exhilarating but challenging- scary even. Exhilarating because it is a record of remarkable growth at St Michael's Aberystwyth. Challenging because of Stuart's laser-like, focus- driven, authentic, uncompromising passion. Nothing quite prepared me for the impact of the final chapter which speaks volumes for the author's integrity. I have had the privilege of ministering briefly at St Michael's and I did encounter a very focussed leader, but at the same time a gracious and vulnerable pastor. A rare combination. Read this book. It is packed with practical wisdom. It will steel your will and warm your heart.
David Bracewell – Director of Zoe ministry

Stuart Bell is a controversial clergyman, never short of a point of view… However, regardless of your churchmanship this is a book well worth reading. After fifty years as an ordained priest he shares a wealth of experience on how church leaders and committed lay people can work, pray and live together to build up churches… Above all it is an insight into a personal, spiritual journey.
Brian Griffiths – Baron Griffiths of Fforestfach

Stuart has distilled a career's worth of wisdom into this volume, which is immensely readable, forthright and practical, especially for anyone in church leadership. He writes with compelling honesty and humility- I wish I could have read this book when I first began in ministry. There are foundational principles here which are well worth the attention of church leaderships everywhere.
Clive Orchard – Team Leader, Ffald y Brenin

Stuart Bell has done the Church a great service by writing the book 'Recovering His Reputation'. It is refreshingly personal, so that the reader is drawn into a sense of travelling with Stuart through each chapter and subject–matter. Yet the personal element is constantly balanced and from time to time challenged by issues of principle and conviction. The book records a lifetime of ministry and mission in which Stuart has been striving to interpret and apply Biblical teaching to contemporary society, with many encouraging results. The whole book is well worth reading. In particular, his engagement with issues of leadership, conflict resolution and evangelism - subjects on which the church at large has in our generation been somewhat flat-footed – will be of help to many readers.

Patrick Mansel Lewis – Chairman of the St Teilo's Trust

Recovering His Reputation:

The Ministry of a Late Developer

Stuart R. Bell

Recovering His Reputation: the ministry of a late developer
©2022 Stuart R Bell

First published in 2022

The right of Stuart R Bell to be identified as the Author of this Work has been asserted by him in accordance with the Copyright, Designs and Patents Act 1988.

All rights reserved. No part of this publication may be reproduced, stored in a retrieval system, or transmitted in any form or by any means, electronic, mechanical, photocopying, recording or otherwise, without the prior consent of the author, nor be otherwise circulated in any form of binding or cover other than that which it is published and without a similar condition being imposed on the subsequent purchaser.

All Scripture quotations, unless otherwise indicated, are taken from the Holy Bible, New International Version®, NIV® Copyright ©1973, 1978, 1984, 2011 by Biblica, Inc.™ Used by permission of Zondervan. All rights reserved worldwide. www.zondervan.com The "NIV" and "New International Version" are trademarks registered in the United States Patent and Trademark Office by Biblica, Inc. Scripture quotations marked (ESV) are from The ESV® Bible (The Holy Bible, English Standard Version) ®, copyright ©2001 by Crossway, a publishing ministry of Good News Publishers. Used by permissions. All rights reserved. Scripture quotations marked (KJV) are from The Authorised (King James Bible) Version. Rights on the Authorized Version in the United Kingdom are vested in the Crown. Reproduced by permission of the Crown's patentee, Cambridge University Press. Scripture quotations marked (NIrV), are taken from the Holy Bible, New International Reader's Version ® NIrV® Copyright ©1995, 1996, 1998, 2014 by Biblica, Inc.™ Used by permission of Zondervan. All rights reserved worldwide. www.zondervan.com The "NIrV" and "New International Reader's Version" are trademarks registered in the United States Patent and Trademark Office by Biblica, Inc. Scripture quotations marked (ERV) are taken from the Holy Bible: Easy-to-Read Version (ERV), International Edition ©2013, 2016 by Bible League International and used by permission. All Scripture marked with the designation "GW" is taken from GOD'S WORD®™. ©1995, 2003, 2013, 2014, 2019, 2020 by God's Word to the Nations Mission Society. Used by permission.

Every effort has been made to source all quoted material, and gain permission to quote. The author will be pleased to rectify any errors or omissions at the earliest opportunity.

Cover design: ©Prudence Bell, 2022. Used with permission.
Photograph of St Michael's Church Aberystwyth superimposed upon the East window depicting the Ascension by A O Hemmings, 1890 in the same church, is used in the cover design with permission from the Revd. Mark Ansell, Area Dean and Vicar of Aberystwyth.
The Cross and Dove design on title page and cover had been created from the stained glass window of St Francis and St Cecilia in the Side Chapel in St Michael's Church Aberystwyth, designed by Laurence Lee Stevens, 1957; and was the logo of St Michael's Church up to 2014. Used with permission from the Revd. Mark Ansell, Area Dean and Vicar of Aberystwyth.

In memory of

Bertie Lewis

mentor, friend and confidant.
one-time Dean of St Davids Cathedral

Contents

Preface ii

Introduction 1

Getting there from here 5

Taking the knee 16

Recovering His Reputation 29

Making disciples 43

Permission refusers 54

Values and aspirations 61

Growth ceilings: paper, glass or reinforced concrete 73

Breaking the rules 80

Received wisdom about staff 96

Evangelise or die 105

Stopping the revolving door syndrome 119

Decision Making – who says? 131

Resolving conflict 146

Out of the pulpit 155

Self care 168

Into retirement 177

An accidental prophecy? 188

i

Preface

At the beginning of the Coronavirus lockdown (March 2020), I received an email from a friend mentioning a conversation he had been having. This is what he wrote, 'Bob said how important it could be for experienced colleagues in ministry to pass on their wisdom to the next generation. This was in the context of talking about you in particular! We did wonder whether you could make use of your enforced idleness to write something - maybe even record something - about lessons you have learned in ministry which could be of help to others. How about it?'

My reply went like this, 'Firstly, I'm not idle! Secondly, any attempt I've ever made to write something (apart from articles and sermons) has come to nothing. I've never felt any guidance nor had a call to do so.'

The slight hint of pique in my reply came from the fact that I am a driven man and have never been bored or without something to do since childhood. Idleness is something I know nothing about.

In addition to that, some thirty years ago I had the idea of writing something very simple on the crucifixion of Jesus which could be used amongst enquirers and new Christians. This was in the days of Word Processors, so I took our Amstrad away with me for the day to our static caravan and I completed the outline of the book and wrote several chapters. It was superb. My fingers flew across the keyboard. It was inspired. It was going to be of immense value to the cause of Christ. Thousands would be converted by reading it. Then I pressed the save key and lost the lot! I've not been very enthusiastic about writing a book ever since.

Yet strangely once the idea from that email had been planted in my mind it began to take root. I even had a working title for the book, *'I wouldn't do that again'*. Much of my 'wisdom' has been burned into my soul through the embarrassment of making mistakes and if anyone wanted to read a book about my mistakes then I would have plenty of material to offer them. I made a few notes on one side of

A4, put it in my in-tray to keep it current and went back to getting on with the list of 28 outstanding jobs which needed to be done in the house and the garden, until some weeks later when I received another email 'out of the blue.'

This one was from the French husband of a university friend from over fifty years ago, Elie Ferraro from Avignon. He is not a man I know very well and we have rarely communicated. Here's the text of what he wrote, 'After hesitating several days I [Elie] decided to tell you about a dream I had of a conversation with you. Perhaps it can be of some encouragement or help now or later or ... never!! In my dream we were speaking about a big project around sharing on a large scale your experience of teaching the Bible message and its content that you have accumulated over a life of service. But the scale of the need and the feeling of your inadequacy was preventing you from starting. I told you in my dream (so clearly that this awoke me, and I remember it nearly a week after). "Don't be afraid, you have and will have enough to feed the entire world." '[1]

Should we listen to such dreams? There are those who say that we should not and that the only source of firm guidance that we should rely upon is the teaching of the Scriptures. Yet, of course, both in the Old Testament and in the New we find repeated examples of the way that the Lord has guided his people through dreams. Surely this was not to be ignored?

If the first email to me concerning writing a book was a hint, it seems to me that the second email about Elie's dream was a command. Get on with it. So here in obedience to what I believe to be the promptings of the Spirit is a reflection on the ministry of a late developer. It would not have been written without Elie's dream and his obedience in telling me about it.

29 June 2021 was the fiftieth anniversary of my ordination. Not a day has passed without me enjoying and experiencing the company and support of Prudence, my wife. She has been entirely committed to the work of the ministry at my side. She has exercised a ministry

---

[1] Email received on 10 May 2020.

as a lay woman in her own right. She could have pursued her own career as a qualified Occupational Therapist, but she chose right at the very beginning to work alongside me in an unsalaried, and often unrecognised capacity. The one gift of hers, which I have valued more than any other, has been her gift of encouragement. That is one of her primary gifts, and it has kept me in the battle over the years and has kept me sane. She has read, re-read and advised in so many ways in the production of this script because the story which is recorded here is as much hers as it is mine.

Jean Morgan was my PA for a number of years in St Michael's Aberystwyth and I have to admit that at retirement she was the one person I missed most of all. I had relied on her so much for so long, but it has been a pleasure to work with her once again on the text of this book. She has done some of the historical research for me and has provided me with some of the background information that I had forgotten. Others who have helped with additional information include Robin Morris and Hannah Green. Their record keeping has been truly remarkable.

This book would never have seen the light of day if it had not been for Will Strange and Bob Capper who have been friends for many decades. Through them the seed of writing the book was planted in my mind in that original email and they together with Will Gibbons have both read the script and commented on it so very helpfully.

David Ceri Jones is Reader in Early Modern History at Aberystwyth University as well as a valued member of St Michael's Church during my time as Rector. He has brought editorial shape to my final script along with a number of important historical and theological observations which have been incorporated into the text.

None of what is written in this book could have happened without the loving, loyal support of so many of my clergy colleagues and co-leaders in the Rectorial Benefice of Aberystwyth, all of whom remain unnamed. I made the decision at the outset that if I was to name one then I would have to name them all and the associated dangers of that were immense. All I need to say to them is, 'You know who you are.' Thank you so very much.

But without the members of the congregation in St Michael's Aberystwyth (and the other congregations where we have served over the years) there would be no story to tell. It is their devotion to the Lord, their prayers, their example, their godliness, their quiet unassuming love which has been such an inspiration. Your names and faces and personal stories remain in our hearts. Your love for us is gladly returned to you.

At this point having thanked everyone, authors usually say that any faults or mistakes in the remaining text are theirs and theirs alone. I wanted to say the reverse and tell my readers that if they found anything wrong in this book then I can quickly find someone else to blame! In actual fact those who have read this script in advance of publication have challenged me on a number of issues, and there have been some lively debates as a result, but now I have to admit to all who read these chapters that I alone am responsible for what has been written.

Stuart R Bell
April 2022

Introduction

There's an old illustration for preachers which tells the story of the bright young banking executive who has just been promoted at the age of 35 to a senior position. He's excited by what lies ahead but also more than a little daunted by the prospect of failing to make a success of this demanding role. He settles on the idea of going to see the executive whom he had replaced and who had just retired in order to get some guidance in his new post. This senior man is highly respected and had enjoyed a distinguished career.

In opening the conversation the young man begins by saying, 'I've come to see you in order to learn from your experience and for you to give me some pointers which will allow me to succeed in the years to come.' The older man replies, 'You need to make mistakes.' To which the younger man replies, 'But that's precisely why I've come to see you. I want to avoid making mistakes, how do I do that?' Back comes the reply, 'To avoid making mistakes you need to make some mistakes.'

There's deep wisdom here. Practical wisdom to be heeded. As a young man finishing my three years as a curate in the west Wales town of Aberaeron, I was advised by a more senior colleague, 'You need to go out into the country for a few years now and make all of your mistakes. Then you can move parishes and begin your life's work.' That sounds pretty cynical and rather dismissive of ministry in a rural context but again there's hidden wisdom in those words. The more the mistakes, the more the experience. The more the experience, the more the wisdom. The more the wisdom, the more the chance of success. Of course, this assumes that the mistakes are harnessed and learned from and not repeated over and over again.

Making mistakes is a deeply painful process and some of us never get over them. They crush us, disappoint us and haunt us to such an extent that our ministries never recover. All of us as we make our mistakes need to find not just that place of forgiveness from the Lord, but also forgiveness from the people we have wounded and hurt. Perhaps most of all we need to learn to forgive ourselves so that we don't spend the rest of our lives full of recrimination towards ourselves for our immaturity or lack of wisdom. In its root that ongoing self accusation, of which I am so very familiar, is a pride issue. I'm embarrassed by me, and it's painful. What really has happened is that my pride has been hurt because I have let myself down and in order to find that really deep peace of soul I need to repent of my inner conceit.

The godly response to our mistakes is repentance. Repentance is motivational. It has movement within it. It makes the necessary changes under the power of the Spirit of God. If the prodigal son had only felt regret as he was feeding the pigs, then he would have continued in that career for the rest of his life. If he had only felt remorse, then there would have been no change in him. He would have felt depressed about himself and his occupation, but he would have stayed where he was. But when he repented he said, 'I will arise and go to my father and say to him, I have sinned against heaven and before you.'[1] That was the moment of progress. That's where our mistakes should take us. I did it. I am the guilty one. I am deeply sorrowful for what I did. I'm asking for forgiveness and the power to be different the next time around.

This has repeatedly been the hallmark of my progress towards ministerial maturity. I suppose it is inevitable that this should be the pattern for leaders and yet it is much more desirable that someone else should have the pain and that I should have the benefit of their mistakes to save me from the embarrassment of making them myself.

We are supposed to climb on the shoulders of those who have gone before us so that we can stand taller and rise higher than they did. In retirement many church leaders feel that they are ready to start their ministry rather than to bring it to an end. If only I could have been born old! If only I could have started out with all this acquired wisdom, then we could have achieved so much more.

---

[1] Luke 15:18.

The purpose of this book is to share my embarrassment and pain with any who will read these chapters so that they don't have to learn the lessons which came at such a cost to me. I'm pleased to say that most of the time this embarrassment and pain took me forwards, upwards, onwards, further, though the scars are still there. Although the experiences might appear to be negative yet because they could be harnessed under the direction of the Spirit, by the grace of God they took me in a mostly positive direction with some thrilling outcomes.

So this book is not intended to be a history of St Michael's Church Aberystwyth nor of the Rectorial Benefice. A history book would have to mention all five churches including Holy Trinity, St Mair, St Anne's and Llanychaearn. It would give details about their particular emphases and the nature of the ministry that they exercised. It would have a chronology of what happened and when. There would also be a list of all of the clergy some of whom were my colleagues and friends who had served these various congregations over the years.

I have nothing to say either about church buildings and their repair and renovation which occupied too much of my time in ministry. The third St Michael's church, which is the present one, was completed in 1890 and should never have been built from soft Yorkshire sandstone. By the time that I became Rector, the building was already worn out and crumbling. We should have been courageous enough to abandon it, which was the recommendation of one of our bishops at the time. In the not too distant future someone will have to take the tough decision to demolish it or otherwise it will cost multiple millions to hand it on to the next generation.

But these are not the purposes of this book. I simply want to speak as a late developer and to help others to avoid some of the pain of ministry in a local church so that they can go further and go faster. This is mostly a record of my years in Aberystwyth slice by slice. I have been deliberately selective about the themes which I have included. They are the ones which were the most important to me, and which contributed the most to the development of my ministry and the growth of St Michael's. So anyone who is looking for a full overview of the life and work of a minister will find this book unsatisfying. I hope, however, that there is sufficient here to stimulate and motivate others to harness their mistakes, and mine, and climb higher.

Only historians will be interested in what happened when, whereas all ministers who want to mature in their ministry will be interested in what others have learned through their mis-judgements, wrong calls and bad decisions; yet also through the promptings of the Spirit and the guidance of Almighty God himself.

Under God, St Michael's Church in Aberystwyth became the largest Anglican church in the whole of Wales. Whilst others were planning for decline, we were planning for growth and seeing it happen. Whilst others were closing buildings, we were looking for more space and were purchasing new accommodation. Whilst others were reducing their staff we were recruiting more. Whilst others were constrained by lack of finance, we were seeking to release greater resources still.

At a church weekend away in 2005 David Bracewell, who at the time was Vicar of St Saviour's Guildford, lay before us the challenge to move from success to significance. I believe that during those decades this was something which happened before our eyes and the legacy of it remains to this day. So here is some of that progress recorded step by step. There is a logic, in my mind at least, to the way that the subject of each chapter follows on from the previous one, but at the same time each of them stands alone as relevant to the church as it is today.

Getting there from here

'In their hearts human beings plan their lives. But the LORD decides where their steps will take them' (Proverbs 16: 9) [NIrV].

I felt just like Rehoboam in April 1988 when I became Rector of Aberystwyth taking over just a fortnight after the departure of Solomon, otherwise known as Archdeacon Bertie Lewis.

King Solomon in ancient times had extended the borders of Israel further than anyone before or since. He was famous for his wisdom, for his leadership and for his reign of peace. His son and successor, Rehoboam, when he was crowned king succeeded in splitting the nation into two through some insensitive and immature decisions. What his father, Solomon and his grandfather, David had built over their lifetimes had been ripped apart within months. The man was a fool.

Bertie Lewis had a remarkable ministry in Aberystwyth between 1980 and 1988. It was going to be a challenge to succeed him. When he began his ministry in St Michael's there was a congregation of seventy in the morning and thirty in the evening. When he left there were 200 in the morning and over 100 in the evening.

He was a multi-talented minister and one of those omni-competent clergy that youngsters like me at the time tried to emulate, but frequently failed to do so. I had served as his curate for three years so knew him well. He was good at everything. He was compelling in the pulpit, was an effective evangelist, was a natural leader, was musical, was excellent at raising money, renovated church buildings wherever he went and much more. He had charisma, yet when he arrived in Aberystwyth, whilst he was a clear evangelical, he was definitely not a Charismatic.

Fairly soon after being there he invited Canon Michael Green to come for the weekend and part of the programme included offering a Saturday morning meeting to local clergy and church leaders from the area. I was present at that meeting myself, being in ministry in the parish of Aberaeron just fifteen miles away.

Michael Green spoke with his usual vigour about how a church which had been renewed by the Holy Spirit might look. He commended the need for a fresh work of the Spirit in our lives in order to build an effective church. There was a Q&A session to finish and then people left. What happened subsequently I heard from Bertie Lewis himself.

There was a young student present at that meeting from the local Presbyterian Theological College. He asked Michael Green to pray that he might receive the fullness of the Spirit. Michael was not going to do the praying alone, so he called Bertie Lewis over, together with the retired Bishop of St Davids, John Richards, who was also present. They gathered around the young man and began to pray for him, and he in his turn spontaneously began to pray in tongues as the Holy Spirit came upon him. Bertie Lewis was staggered by what he was witnessing. It was so genuine and unaffected and was just what the Acts of the Apostles recorded.

Over that weekend Bertie sought the same blessing from the Holy Spirit for himself and received it. When I saw him the following week I was speaking to a different man. As we were talking, he had to leave the room on one occasion in order to weep and recover himself. The change of spiritual temperature which was already taking place in St Michael's Aberystwyth under his evangelical ministry now accelerated. It was said that the fastest growing church in the area was the neighbouring parish of Llanbadarn Fawr as so many people were leaving because they could not agree with the new regime, but they were being replaced still more quickly by new Christians, many of whom were being converted through Bertie's ministry. There is still a biography waiting to be written on the influence of this great man. So here is Rehoboam, me, in his youth, wondering whether he is going to be able to succeed Solomon and take the church forward or whether he'll just be a fool and let it all slip through his fingers.

That might have been my fear, but there are plenty of other examples of succession in the Bible which worked out differently. Moses had his Joshua. Different men for different tasks. One to bring the Children of Israel out of Egypt and lead them through the wilderness, the other to bring them into the promised land and get them settled. Elijah had his Elisha who prayed for a double portion of the Spirit's anointing and received it. There was no slackening of spiritual power and effectiveness as one succeeded the other. In fact, the number of recorded miracles performed by Elisha was precisely double those performed by Elijah. He received what he had prayed for.

Maybe Solomon and Rehoboam was the wrong model for me, even though it felt like that at the time. Maybe the succession would have been better compared to Paul and Apollos? Paul had planted and Apollos watered, but it was God who gave the increase.[2] In fact on reflection that is exactly the way that things turned out.

'The clearer the call, the tougher the task'. This statement contains an enormous amount of truth. Wherever we are in ministry there are going to be problems. In some places it will be the problems of failure and in other places the problems of success; in still others a mixture of both. The conviction which holds us in place when the problems become overwhelming is that to leave would be disobedience and to cave in under the problems would be unbelief. God has called me here and I will stay and see this through. It is only this kind of resolve which will keep us stable, committed and immovable.

Humanly speaking, I had four significant advantages in facing this tough task of succeeding Bertie Lewis as the Rector of Aberystwyth. Firstly, I knew that I was called to ordained leadership. As a boy at Hele Road Baptist Church in Torquay I had heard the minister, David Abernethie, explain in a morning sermon that Jesus had died on a cross for me. The sulky twelve-year-old who had turned up reluctantly at church that morning went home with a changed attitude. So much so that I went voluntarily to the evening service

---

[2] 1 Corinthians 3:6.

which was followed by their youth fellowship. The cross, like the barb on the fishing hook, had penetrated my soul and has never left. It has held me fast.

That was the beginning of the ups and downs of any teenage youngster following the Lord. My enthusiasm for spiritual things was like the temperature chart at the bottom of the bed of a sick hospital patient. It was a series of constant spikes, up one minute and down the next. An enthusiastic Billy Graham slipping Christian tracts into the desks of my friends one minute and the next joining in the same dirty conversations as the rest of them.

I had the offer of being baptised in the Baptist church, but they had one unsettling custom which was to ask each candidate to speak about their conversion and their faith. I couldn't do that because I knew I wasn't walking consistently with the Lord at that time. However, when I was given the opportunity to be baptised in the Anglican church with no questions being asked, I accepted that invitation. So at the age of fourteen I had a private baptism by sprinkling and that was followed by confirmation. The vicar made a strange remark to my mother at my baptism which still stays with me. He told her, 'I'm not giving you a baptism certificate for Stuart because you'll only need it if he gets ordained.' Somehow that smiley off-hand remark stuck with me, and even though I was still such an inconsistent disciple nonetheless I couldn't escape a growing impression that the Lord wanted me in the ordained ministry.

It was in my second year in the sixth form at school, aged seventeen, that my commitment to Christ crystallized. I was becoming increasingly challenged inwardly that either I was going for this discipleship seriously or I was going to give it up altogether. I couldn't continue to live this half life of being a Christian on the outside and being something else on the inside; that had already been going on for years. Every afternoon after school I went into a local church building that was unlocked and I prayed that the Lord would accept me. I did this for a whole week from Monday through to the Friday, and by the Friday afternoon I knew that I would never ever have to pray that prayer again. Paul says that God's Spirit witnesses with ours that we are children of God, and that is exactly what had happened.[3] At the end of that week I had a certainty and assurance that has never gone away since then.

Secondly, along with that serious and decisive commitment to Christ went a willingness to offer myself for ordained leadership. Even in my years of half-heartedness I prayed occasionally, and as I sat my 'O' level exams I asked the Lord for a sign as to whether or not I should be ordained. When my exam results came back I wasn't the only person to be rather taken aback by the mark for my Religious Knowledge paper – 90%! None of my other marks came anywhere near that.

The question arose as to whether or not I should go back to the Baptists which was where I had first heard the Gospel or whether I should stay with the Anglicans who asked no questions when I agreed to be baptised and confirmed. Paul's advice concerning staying in the situation you are in when you are called seemed relevant to my circumstances. He was referring to slaves being converted and whether or not they should try to obtain their freedom, and to whether or not non-Jews who were converted should be circumcised. His advice was, 'each one should retain the place in life that the Lord assigned to him.'[4] I was now in the Anglican church, so staying in the Anglican church pursuing ordained leadership within the same denomination seemed the best way forward.

Thirdly, if I had become certain of my Christian faith whilst still in school, it was not until I was at theological college in Bristol that I became certain of the Lord's call to ministry in the Church in Wales.

For two years before going to college we had been living in Coventry. It was during that time that Pru and I got married and she joined me in a lifetime of committed ministry. We had met whilst I was reading theology in Exeter University and she was training as an Occupational Therapist in St Loyes College in the same city. By

---

[3] Romans 8:16.
[4] 1 Corinthians 7:17-24.

this time we were in Coventry together to gain some experience of life before going forward for training and then ordination. The selection panel for ministry had concluded that I needed some opportunity to see life in a secular context rather than go from school to university to theological college to ordination. That was a wise recommendation.

From the Midlands we took advantage of exploring mid-Wales which was so easy to access. On one hitchhiking holiday we stayed in Bala enjoying B&B accommodation at the local policeman's home. He was a member of Capel Tegid in the town and spoke to us of the memories of the 1904 Welsh revival which still lingered in the community. He admitted that the sound of the revival remained in the hymns and songs but that the reality of the revival had departed by then (1969). It occurred as a rather romantic idea that it would be great to come to Wales and try to do something about that. The feelings were compounded by attending an entirely lifeless English language service in one of the chapels in the town on that summer Sunday morning.

Like anything from the Lord, once the idea has begun to take root then it simply won't leave you alone (and still hasn't more than five decades later on). Over the months there was an increasing conviction for both Pru and I that Wales was to be the place where we would serve the Lord. We arrived at this conclusion independently and yet jointly. At the time although we didn't know it, this was going to be something of a homecoming for Pru. In doing some research into her family history she discovered that her great-grandmother came originally from St Davids in Pembrokeshire, that she was a first language Welsh speaker and that she was martyred in the Boxer Rebellion in Taiyuan in China.[5]

---

[5] This story is told in, Prudence Bell with Ronald Clements *Lives from a Black Tin Box: Martyrs of the Boxer Rebellion, their Chinese Church today, and the power of prayer* (Milton Keynes: Authentic 2014).

A decision had to be made concerning a parish placement during my long vacation at Tyndale Hall Theological College[6] in 1970. If we were really going to pursue ordination into the Church in Wales then there was only one direction for us to go and that was to Bill Lewis, a former student at Tyndale who was ministering very effectively in the small country parish of Letterston in Pembrokeshire.

Whilst we were there for my three-week placement and with Bill's encouragement, we began to explore the possibility of being a curate in the St Davids diocese. Remarkably, within that short period of time I was able to see the Director of Ordinands and then attend an interview with the training committee of the Diocese.

One of the lovely things about being young and innocent is that you can miss the nuance of a question. During the interview one of the issues raised by a member of the committee focussed on why I thought that there were so few people from my training college working in Wales. In fact, there was only one, Bill Lewis, with whom I was spending those three weeks. It wasn't until afterwards that I realised that the theological flavour of Tyndale Hall, Bristol, which was evangelical and Low Church was not much appreciated in the diocese or in the wider Church in Wales. However, unbeknown to the man who bowled me the googly, as Bishop John Richards showed me to the door he whispered in my ear, 'We need more evangelicals like you in this diocese'! That was my welcome to ministry in the Church in Wales.

Having been accepted into the diocese of St Davids it was then a matter of finding a vicar willing to take me on as a curate. I had a first conversation with Bertie Lewis (later Rector of Aberystwyth) who was ministering in the parish of Aberaeron at the time. His response was that he could not offer me a post as he needed someone who could speak Welsh fluently. His parish was strongly bilingual and there were Welsh services as well as bilingual services on a weekly basis. I explored other options in the south of Pembrokeshire which is monoglot English speaking, but

---

[6] Tyndale Hall, Clifton Theological College and Dalton House amalgamated to become Trinity College Bristol in 1971.

simultaneously I began learning Welsh with the Bristol Welsh Society.

In the early months of 1971 my options of a curacy in South Pembrokeshire which had been tentatively held out to me came to nothing. At a single stroke it appeared as though the door which was opening had been closed, and then completely unexpectedly I had a letter from Bertie Lewis asking where I had got to in finding a curacy and what my current competence was in Welsh. He interviewed me on Easter Monday and that day our future was fixed. I would be ordained in St Davids Cathedral on Saturday 29 June 1971 and our ministry in Wales was about to begin.

If my call to ministry was certain and so too our call to work in Wales, there was something else that happened on the morning of my ordination which was a triple lock of confirmation that this was the right course for me. The ecclesiastical procession had formed up in the cathedral and moved off. The choir was ahead of us and then behind it were all of the men who were about to be ordained, ten of us. Then behind us came all of the clergy who had come from across the diocese for the occasion. As we came down the steps from the transept into the nave, I heard a voice over my shoulder which said 'This is the way, walk in it.' Those of course, are words from the prophet Isaiah. 'Your ears will hear a voice behind you, saying "This is the way, walk in it." '[7] The voice was so clear that I looked over my shoulder to see who was speaking to me.

A certain call to ordained ministry, a certain call to work in Wales and a certain voice from heaven. These were all massive privileges. What more could a rather fearful new Rector need as he started ministry in Aberystwyth seventeen years later? One thing he most certainly could do with was plenty of ministerial experience, and this had been provided firstly by Bertie Lewis who was my training incumbent in Aberaeron. From there we had moved to the village of Llangeler near Llandysul in the Teifi Valley. There were three churches in this rural parish, all of them predominantly Welsh speaking. It was then that I fully realised how alive and vibrant the

[7] Isaiah 30:21.

Welsh language is. At first I couldn't believe that people would speak Welsh on the phone! It's that much more difficult when you can't lip-read as you listen.

But not only is Welsh the language of everyday life for so many people, it is also the language of the soul. It is a language of prayer and of worship and of the heart. Some would argue (and I agree with them) that the soul of the nation, its conscience, its memory, its history, its heart is in the Welsh language. The soul needs to be addressed in its own language. For that reason, I continued my Welsh language studies and the congregations were wonderfully patient with me, so that six years later as we moved away I carried with me a Welsh accent that is identifiably from the Teifi Valley.

It was here in a small rural community that I made so many of my early mistakes, just as was expected. I tried to bring a townie's agenda to the countryside. I tried to make things move as fast as I had become used to in Aberaeron. I tried making rapid decisions on my own without sufficient reference to the wardens and church committees. I misunderstood the culture and brought an Englishness with me which was not helpful. There were small and upsetting mistakes like refusing an 'Englyn' which is a Bardic inscription for a gravestone because I didn't understand the long-standing tradition of their use on Welsh tombs.

There were greater mismatches of expectation when I succeeded in arranging for the building of our redundant church school to be given back to the parish. According to the deeds the land on which the school was built had been donated by Lampeter College. I spoke to the Chairman of the College Council who happened to be the same Bishop John Richards and he assured me that the College would waive their title to the land and give the building to the parish. I turned up at the next PCC meeting and announced my news expecting to be applauded on all sides but one of the men said 'First of all I propose that we take a vote to decide whether or not we will accept this offer.' That was a hard lesson in corporate decision making.

But two of our three children were born while we were there and one of them was named after the smallest of the churches. By the time that we were preparing to leave, our family was well known in the communities and there was a sense of ownership of us which still lingers decades later on.

Our ministry in Llangeler was followed by a further eight years back in the parish of Aberaeron where I had served my curacy. Some twelve years before that time, my wife and I had stood on the quayside of the harbour whilst on holiday with the sailing boats riding high on a full tide and looked across at the church and said to one another, 'Wouldn't it be great to be a vicar here?' Now I was. We had a second bite of the cherry, first as curate and now as vicar.

Once again there were three churches, once again there was plenty of ministry in the Welsh language, and once again there was growth both spiritual and numerical.[8] But at the end of eight years (early 1988) I began to feel that the people were starting to say 'no' to me. I felt that I had lost something in terms of leadership and influence and that it was time to look elsewhere. We began measuring ourselves against other parishes in the diocese which would have been 'the next step up' in terms of size and 'importance'. However, unexpectedly I received a phone call from Bertie Lewis asking me to visit him in the Rectory in Aberystwyth.

I had a complete surprise when he told me that since he had become Archdeacon it was becoming almost impossible for him to do that work and continue as Rector of Aberystwyth. It had already been arranged for him to move to the small rural parish of Nevern in the south of the archdeaconry and he wanted me to be his successor in Aberystwyth. The fact that we had already sensed a loosening of our roots in Aberaeron fitted perfectly with such a proposal. In due course my application was submitted to the Diocesan Nominations Board and I was appointed; the first horse in a one-horse race. No-one else had applied.

---

[8] Some of the story of those years is told in John Richardson, *Ten Rural Churches* (Eastbourne: MARC, 1988), pp. 135-50.

There were two particularly amusing incidents in my past which I couldn't help recalling as we prepared for the move. One of our family holidays had brought us to Aberystwyth when I was a child and my only memory from that holiday was sitting on the South Beach and getting tar on my trousers for which I was in big trouble. That had clearly coloured my view of the town, as when one of my friends from the sixth form at school was submitting his application for a university place at Aberystwyth I said to him, 'What on earth do you want to go to that place for?' Now here we were taking on a massive new challenge but with a certain faith, a certain call to ordained leadership, a certain call to Wales and seventeen years of practical parish ministry.

'The clearer the call, the tougher the task'. We weren't just arriving in Aberystwyth without any kind of preparation or experience. God is an economist and he wastes nothing from our personal history, even the hard and difficult times he weaves into our characters and into our ministries allowing us to serve others with compassion and understanding. But being Rector of Aberystwyth was going to be a very tough task indeed involving the leadership of five churches, a substantial ordained and lay team, chaplaincy to the university, chaplaincy to the General Hospital and an extensive ministry to the tourists during the summer. A big and demanding job. Thank the Lord for the clear call.

Thinking moment

- How has the Lord used your past, including your mistakes, in your present service for him?

- Is there anything from your past which has not been used yet? Is there a way that you could see it becoming significant in the future?

Taking the knee

'Hear from heaven their prayer and their plea, and uphold their cause' (II Chronicles 6:35).

'Taking the knee' as an act of protest began in the United States with an NFL player Colin Kaepernick on 26 August 2016. Instead of standing for the American national anthem as he was expected to do and place a hand over his heart, he bent to the ground on one knee as a protest against racial oppression.

From ancient times men and women of God have 'taken the knee' before the Lord. Not on one knee but on two. Not in order to make a protest but as an act of worship, submission and of supplication. Very simply they have prayed, and their prayers have been accompanied by a physical posture; kneeling on the ground.

Prayer is a mystery which will only be fully understood when we get to heaven. Jesus was specific with his disciples when he commanded them to pray. He told 'his disciples a parable to show them that they should always pray and not give up.'[1] He said again, 'Ask and you will receive and your joy will be complete'.[2] In some inexplicable way God uses our prayers in order to accomplish his will.

Experience tells us that it is prayer which makes the difference time and time again. It is prayer which opens doors, prayer which changes people, prayer which moves mountains. The examples of great Christian leaders from the past all demonstrate the same truth. Billy Graham in his autobiography tells of an offer from a benefactor who promised to underwrite his ministry so that he would have no further financial worries. Billy Graham replied, 'I can't accept that. My work is spiritual work. We are getting about 15-20,000 letters a week. Most of those letters have a little money in them, maybe $1 or $5. But every one of those letters is saying, 'We are praying for you.' If they know there's a rich man

---

[1] Luke 18:1.
[2] John 16:24.

underwriting my work, they'll stop praying and my work will take a nosedive. So I can't accept it.'[3] Not many Christian leaders would give that reply.

We can employ the latest techniques, try to imitate the strategies of others, sweat ourselves to a state of dehydration through our efforts but nothing will be accomplished in the kingdom of God without prayer. We can build a kingdom on earth by our own efforts without a doubt; many have already done so, but the kingdom of God will not move forward by a millimetre without prayer.

This really is volume one, chapter one and page one for Christian discipleship and for Christian ministry, but because prayer is so hard we still try to find other ways of accomplishing the work of God. Over the years our prayerlessness has been described in two words, 'practical atheism'. Prayer is all too frequently our last resort rather than our first. This is in stark contrast to the disciples of Jesus who saw the impact of his prayers and wanted to learn his 'secret'. They didn't ask him how to prepare sermons, or how to heal the sick, or how to cast out demons. They knew that the power he possessed came from his prayer life, so they asked him, 'Lord, teach us to pray'.[4]

I was taught from an early stage in my Christian life that having a daily 'quiet time', involving reading the Bible and praying, was essential for spiritual stability and maturity. It was a discipline which was hard won in the early years but with a group of serious-minded Christian students at university it was solidified into a daily pattern of life.

By the time that I met Pru, who was going to be my wife, I was comfortable praying aloud with others and as a result the two of us would pray together every time we met, and have subsequently prayed together almost every day for the rest of our married life.

[3] *Just as I am: the autobiography of Billy Graham* (New York: Harper Collins, 1997), p. 661.
[4] Luke 11:1.

Our pattern is to spend an hour together first thing in the morning with the Bible open for thirty minutes and then to pray for thirty minutes. During our years of full-time ministry our day would begin at 6.30 am whilst now in retirement we begin at the more leisurely time of 7.00 am. Currently we are using a prayer diary, but during our time in the parish I found that too difficult to maintain as we were 'fire fighting' in prayer so much of the time. The daily needs were so great that they absorbed all of our prayer attention.

When Basil Gough, one-time principal of Clifton Theological College in Bristol was instructing his ministerial students about life in the parish he gave a particular piece of advice about prayer. He told his students that when they had a parish of their own the first thing that they should do was to announce a prayer meeting for the following week and that way they would identify the people in the church who were spiritually minded. What sound advice.

We didn't need to do that in Aberystwyth because there were so many people who were already devoted to prayer. Bertie Lewis had already established a weekly prayer meeting which was lay-led. His method of encouraging prayer was 'just do it'. Nike must have been listening!

I hadn't been there long when during a Prayer and Praise meeting on a Tuesday evening I was so excited by my theme that I said that if we were really serious about revival then we'd be meeting at 6 am to pray for it. I was trying to make a point, of course, not being serious. It was just preacher's rhetoric! Except that after the meeting one of the people present came up to me and asked, 'When do we start?' So I announced that we would be meeting at 6 am the following morning and fifteen people turned up. The vestry was electric with prayer. I'd never experienced that level of intensity and faith in a meeting. Things got 'worse' for me before the end because I didn't know how to draw it to a faith-filled conclusion when it was time to go. So instead of finishing with the grace or some other appropriate ending, I slipped away whilst the meeting was in full flow. The leader left! What on earth was I thinking about? I'll never do that again.

Those prayer meetings continued for a period of over five years. They happened three times a week on Mondays, Wednesdays and Fridays. Many of those who came went home afterwards for their own devotional times. Two of the regulars went on to be ordained, one to become a lay reader, one to go to Texas to work with Mercy Ships and another to one of the Central Asian Republics to work with an NGO. The impact of those 6 am prayers have most certainly been recorded in heaven.

Timing a prayer meeting for that early in the morning doesn't suit everyone. Family circumstances, work commitments, or even certain temperaments make such an early start impractical. There were other prayer meetings during the week which were open to everyone on a Wednesday morning at 8 am (followed by breakfast) or a Friday night at 7.30 pm when others could make the effort to be present for intercession and to bring the needs of the church before the Lord. Whilst some might find the mornings rather too difficult for them there were others who thrived in our occasional half nights of prayer when we would leave the church building at midnight.

Most of us, however much we have prayed, however often, for however long, over however many years, rarely feel that we have graduated from the kindergarten in terms of making real progress. All of us feel that we have not prayed enough, we have not been earnest enough, we have not listened enough as we have prayed. It has been too formal, too cold, sometimes too desperate, sometimes too much like a shopping list. And yet Brother Lawrence of *The Practice of the Presence of God* fame brings us great comfort when he writes, 'For many years I was bothered by the thought that I was a failure at prayer. Then one day I realised that I would always be a failure at prayer; and I've got along much better ever since'.[5] We just need to do it. Nike again!

Jesus was rather challenging about prayer because he linked fasting with praying suggesting it would make our prayers still more effective. Instructing his disciples on fasting, Jesus says to them, 'When you fast'.[6] He does not say, 'If you fast.' He's taking it for granted that this spiritual practice is one that his disciples would want to follow themselves. I have always found fasting alone difficult to do, but when we have done it together as a church it has been much easier. From time to time we would proclaim a fast for the congregation especially when one of our members was seriously ill, or we were faced with a big decision or a particular difficulty. Sometimes it was just a single day, sometimes it was a full week. If we had a week's fast then prayer meetings would be held in the church three times a day at normal meal times. As an exercise in declaring our seriousness to heaven over the issues we were praying about this was an excellent statement to one another and to the Lord.

One of the mistakes I made regarding fasting was to try to institutionalise it. In my early years I proclaimed a fast for the church once a month on a regular basis. Initially the proposal had great support and there was energy and enthusiasm for the idea. However, as the months passed it became more of a duty. It lost its sparkle and focus and sense of purpose. It seems to me that when fasting is separated from a particular purpose and exists just for itself then it's much harder for everyone to be engaged. I quietly dropped the monthly announcement and no one said a thing. They must have been so relieved, or perhaps by the end I was the only one who was trying to do it.

One of our men told me that he had the gift of intercession. He could pray for three hours at a stretch and not notice the passing of

---

[5] Quoted in John Ortberg, *The Life You've Always Wanted* (Grand Rapids, MI: Zondervan, 2002), p. 96.
[6] Matthew 6:16ff.

time. That was an unusually heightened gifting but one which we were keen to harness. Over the years we recruited more than a hundred people from our congregation who took our confidential prayer bulletin and they provided detailed prayer support for the life of the church and its members. This was updated weekly and sometimes in an emergency emails would be sent around to ensure that there was prayer support when needed.

If it is true that prayer makes the difference, regrettably it is also true that it is one of the first things to be dropped and neglected in an over-busy church, but we do so at immense cost to the cause of Christ. Samuel Chadwick was a Methodist minister at the turn of the nineteenth century. He entered into a fresh experience of the Holy Spirit later in his ministry and as a consequence he burned all of his old sermons. His comment was that it wasn't until they were burning that he realised how dry they had been! He went on to give this warning to the church. 'Satan dreads nothing but prayer. Activities are multiplied that meditation may be ousted, and organisations increased that prayer may have no chance. The one concern of the devil is to keep the saints from praying. He fears nothing from our prayerless studies, prayerless work, prayerless religion. He laughs at our toil, mocks our wisdom, but trembles when we pray.'[7]

In the small rural church of Llangeler where I had served for those six years I had a look at the service registers to see what had happened in the parish during the period of the 1904/5 Welsh revival. They told the story of the prayer life of the church in a most revealing way. Before the revival began it was recorded that they had an 'Ysgol Gân' (Singing Rehearsal) on a Sunday evening in addition to their morning service. Then when the revival began they had a 'Cwrdd Gweddi' (Prayer Meeting). As the influence of the revival started to wane they had a 'Cwrdd Gweddi ac Ysgol Gân' (Prayer Meeting and Singing Rehearsal) and then after several more months had passed they went back to having the

[7] Quoted in Bob Gordon, *How Much More Shall the Father give the Holy Spirit to them that ask him* (nd), p. 137.

'Ysgol Gân' (Singing Rehearsal) on its own. Such is the way that decline in praying happens if it is not constantly torched up as an important principle for the church.

It is always a compliment to any ministry if the Prince of Darkness shows an interest in what is going on, although it doesn't feel like much of a compliment when the trouble starts. But if we leave the devil alone then he will leave us alone. A dead church, and a prayerless church is a delight to him as no-one will be being converted and no-one will threaten his kingdom. On the other hand, when a live church starts to make serious inroads into his territory it is in his interest to defend it. The life of the Christian is 'swords drawn to the gate.' The battle will continue until we cross over to glory.

Almost from day one in Aberystwyth we were dealing with people who had been involved in various occult practices and were suffering as a result. The very first case we dealt with was in an empty Rectory with bare floorboards because the carpet had not yet been laid. This continued for several years, and then almost suddenly it stopped. I have never understood quite why. Had we slipped back in the sharpness of our discipleship? Was there some unknown sin somewhere? Had the devil himself backed off? We had certainly seen some remarkable successes. Only heaven could answer those questions and we remain in ignorance today as to the reasons why.

However, from time to time St Michael's itself would suffer from what can only be described as a sustained attack from the evil one. The experience of Job is a help in understanding what was happening because during his first period of testing he faced multiple misfortunes which came upon him in close succession over a short period of time. First of all, he had his donkeys stolen by a neighbouring tribe and his servants killed during the raid, then he lost his sheep in a lightning strike and the shepherds were killed too. Then his camels were plundered by yet another tribe before finally all of his children died when their home collapsed onto them during a storm. As if that wasn't enough it was then that understandably his health broke down too. Tragedy followed tragedy. It was a multiplied onslaught, and the author of it all was Satan himself.[8]

We found that there were occasions in the life of St Michael's when we were aware that something was stirring in the congregation which was from the evil one. It would usually be some kind of sustained trouble with multiple misfortunes, just like Job, as one problem followed another in quick succession. As a result, we would call the membership together in order to deal with what was happening.

Sometimes we could simply sense a spiritual slippage in our church life which was widespread and which needed to be confronted head on and dealt with. If it was true that these issues were from the evil one and if we resisted them and him too, then we could expect them to stop. James is very clear in his letter when he says quite simply, 'Resist the devil and he will flee from you'.[9] We were going to resist him corporately, and our expectation was that he would flee.

One such occasion happened in July 2006. As a first response to the problems we were facing I preached on the text 'The one you love is sick'.[10] This was the message reported to Jesus concerning his friend Lazarus. I drew attention to the fact that we had become sick as a church. A malaise had developed in the life of the church which needed to be dealt with. It wasn't as though everything was wrong. On this particular Sunday I began with the things that thrilled the soul; eleven of them - including our recent experience of some deeply tender worship, some Sundays when the prayer ministry team had been overwhelmed by the response, a full church building and continuing strong giving. I wasn't trying to suggest that nothing was right, but rather that some things were wrong. It wasn't that nothing was happening in the church either but rather

---

[8] Job 1:13 – 2:10.
[9] James 4:7.
[10] John 11:3.

that we had slowed down in so many areas of our different ministries.

We were able to identify an unaccountable slippage. Our congregations had peaked twelve months before and some had gone from twice a Sunday to once a Sunday, and others from once a week to every fortnight, and others from every fortnight to once a month. The numbers of people attending our prayer meeting had dropped. There had developed an erratic attendance from about a third of the children in Sunday Club. Once, this was an absolute family priority now it was not. We hadn't got unity in the church either. Not that we had got disunity, but despite prayer and fasting we didn't have unity of mind and purpose.

In addition to that, all of the areas of ministry in the church were facing problems, rather than the blessing they had been enjoying twelve months earlier. In fact, the major growth area in our church at the time was problems. Regularly we were waiting to complete the sentence, 'And today's crisis is...' There was a time in church that all that would be needed would be to put down the ball in the service, or in the prayer meeting, and there'd be a scrum to pick it up and run with it. There would be competition to participate and to verbalise worship or thanksgiving or intercession. People would be tripping over each other to get involved. Now it was just the usual suspects who contributed. We'd become sluggish spiritually.

We had been here before as a church some years earlier. It was just the same then, as though a huge bonfire had been burning in the garden and everything that was in the centre had burnt to ashes, the fire was still burning strongly, but it was now on the edges not at the centre. There's a fantastic African proverb, 'Beware of the ashes!' That was where we were. The fire was in danger of burning out in the centre and needed to be fed with more fuel.

Spiritual problems require spiritual solutions. This is such an important principle. It should be written in capital letters and underlined. Sometimes we are tempted to try to bring human solutions to spiritual problems. We'll call in the specialist advisers, release some funding, approach the problem from a different angle, put some clever people together in a room to come up with a solution, when all that we should be doing is going directly to the Lord and going directly to our spiritual enemy and dealing with him face to face. The solution for us was to deal with these matters in a corporate way as this was an attack on the whole congregation.

On a previous occasion when we had faced similar difficulties we had called the church to prayer specifically at the regular mid-week meeting. During the course of that meeting we focussed our prayer upon reversing the negative influences and resisting the activity of the evil one amongst us. As part of that time together we invited everyone present to leave the building and to encircle it. We joined hands, all 147 (there was a head count) of us and turned inwards towards the church. We prayed simultaneously together, Korean style, for the life of the church and for its deliverance from everything that would harm it. Then we loosed hands and turned around. Joining hands again we faced outwards to the town and interceded for it, again praying Korean style but concluding with the great festal shout, 'Jesus is Lord'.

There was an atmospheric difference about our services on the following Sunday and that continued for months. It was the change of atmosphere which was so remarkable. Instead of things being heavy and burdensome there was a fresh lightness and sense of the Spirit of God at work amongst us. Where previously we had not had a sense of oneness we now had complete unity of heart.

Following the sermon in July 2006 we had yet another Tuesday evening meeting. We used some of the same principles as before facing down the sense of an evil influence upon us and resisting the devil as the Scriptures instruct us to do. Then, on this occasion we left the church building again, but this time we marched around it seven times declaring the victory of the Lord. Mercifully the walls did not come tumbling down at the festal shout (or maybe that wasn't a mercy!). But the darkness did come tumbling down.

Once again there was the very same atmospheric change in the life of the church as a result of this evening of confrontation with the opposition. Instead of saying that 'the one you love is sick' we could now feel the resuscitation which had taken place amongst us. Lazarus was out of the tomb.

John Bunyan in *The Pilgrim's Progress* has a wonderful image of the security of the child of God in the face of evil opposition. Christian is on his way to the Celestial City but his path is blocked by two lions. The prospect of having to try to pass them is terrifying until as he draws closer, he sees that they are chained at the neck and he is able to pass between them safely. They can roar and he can feel their breath, but they cannot devour him.[11]

When the issues are spiritual they need to be dealt with spiritually. When the issues are corporate then they need to be dealt with corporately. This 'facing down' of evil was a feature of our church's prayer life every couple of years. It could not be predicted in advance, nor was it part of the timetable of our church's calendar, but it was a real experience and something that was absolutely necessary with which to be engaged.

If we needed to deal with these matters corporately from time-to-time we also needed to deal with them privately in our own personal spiritual lives too. The saying is that the devil goes seven times around the parsonage for every one time he goes around the parish. That certainly could be confirmed from our experience. At times of heightened spiritual progress in the church there would often be some kind of push back in our own personal circumstances. There is a hidden cost to church growth which the leadership has to be prepared for and has to bear.

Roy Hession, the British evangelist and author put his finger on the issue when he quoted these insightful words.

---

[11] John Bunyan, *The Pilgrim's Progress* (1678), edited by Roger Pooley (London: Penguin, 1965), p. 78.

> Wherever you ripe fields behold
> Waving to God their sheaves of gold,
> Be sure some corn of wheat has died,
> Some soul has there been crucified,
> Someone has wrestled, wept and prayed
> And fought hell's legions undismayed.[12]

The minister's marriage and family are frequently used as the target by our spiritual opponent including the minister's children. We need to be aware of this and continually be praying the Lord's protection over them. Most ministers will know what it is like to leave the house for a Sunday service after a furious unresolved argument with either spouse or children or both and having to stand there and lead services and preach. The spiritual battle is not lessened because we are in the Lord's service but rather it is intensified and the more effective our ministry the fiercer will be the opposition. We need to be aware of this and take appropriate measures to protect our families in prayer.

One of the continuing disappointments in these spiritual battles is that sometimes the source of the opposition or criticism can come from within the household of faith. History bears witness to the fact that all too often it is not people from outside the church who cause all the trouble but people inside the church or even the church authorities themselves.

Michael Cassidy, a South African Christian leader and founder of Africa Enterprise, known for his ecumenism and reconciliation ministry writes,

> We will need to repent of what I call SIWs. This is a military term which refers to Self-Inflicted Wounds. This is what happens when a soldier, instead of throwing the grenade at the enemy, allows it to explode in his own hand. He wounds and immobilises himself. This is militarily catastrophic and almost criminal. It is also spiritually so. Nothing is more tragic than

---

[12] Roy Hession, *My Calvary Road* (London: Hodder and Stoughton, 1978), p. 99.

when the church participates in all sorts of acts by which it wounds itself and tears itself down. I don't believe in our own ministry that we have ever had any of our projects or enterprises torn down or immobilised by Marxists, by pagans, by free lovers, by atheists or by Muslims. The only people who have ever torn down any Christian initiatives in which we have personally been involved have been other Christians. And what makes it worse is that when Christians knock each other down they hardly ever do it by frontal assault. It is almost always via the arrow from behind. This is a destructive killer in the church. It is inexcusable.[13]

While these kinds of battles are deeply disappointing our response needs to be one of integrity, we must not respond in kind. Rather we must be the ones who demonstrate the utmost dignity and courage as we call out behaviour which is ungodly and destructive. As a Christian leader said to me recently when we were going through the mill again, 'Keep yourself sweet'. However, we do need to recognise the seat of this kind of opposition and confront it spiritually. Spiritual problems require spiritual solutions. At the ordination of every minister there should be a commissioning for service which includes the sentence, 'Let battle commence!'

Thinking moment

- All of us are failures at prayer, but taking into account our current circumstances how could we improve our prayer discipline and daily devotional rhythm?
- Spiritual problems need to be spiritually addressed, so how should we go about dealing with spiritual opposition when we experience it as a church congregation?

---

[13] Michael Cassidy, *Bursting the Wineskins* (London: Hodder and Stoughton, 1983), p. 232.

Recovering His Reputation

'Where there is no vision, the people perish' (Proverbs 29: 18) [KJV].

One of the features of the life of businesses, charities and other public bodies at the turn of the millennium was to write and publish their vision or mission statements; what they intended to achieve and how they were going to go about it. It was surprising and sometimes amusing to see a mission statement being displayed in a secular business because mission is what the church is meant to be about whilst commercial enterprises exist to make money. We were being beaten at our own game.

This enthusiasm for vision statements and mission statements transferred over to the churches and many put on paper the reason for their existence and the objectives that they were working towards. They published them everywhere by including brief strap lines on their letter headings and newsletters and advertised them on their notice boards. However, those who belonged to the Lord and who were aiming to minister from the Scriptures to their congregations already had a fairly clear idea of where they were going, what they wanted to do and how they were going to achieve their objectives.

If you were to have asked me as the new Rector on the block what my vision was for St Michael's Aberystwyth then I would have been able to tell you in one word – growth. This surely must be the visionary enterprise of every minister unless a congregation is facing exceptional circumstances. Jesus said, 'I will build my church.'[1] He did not promise to preside over its closure or its demise or its funeral. Jesus was and still is looking for growth. Growth in his kingdom. Growth in the number of his disciples. Growth in the spiritual maturity of his people. Growth in godliness and growth in holiness. Growth! If he was looking out for that and

---

[1] Matthew 16:18.

was making it happen, then I should be looking out for that and should want to make it happen as well.

The way that young people were discipled when I became a fully committed Christian was to teach them to pray, to encourage them to read the Bible, to establish a personal devotional life, and to learn how to lead another person to Christ. We were taught the ABCD of the Gospel. Admit that you are a sinner. Believe that Jesus died to deal with your sin. Consider the cost of following him. Decide to give your life to Christ and invite him in.

Tract distribution was something that we did as young Christians as a matter of course, and regularly there were open air services. In Torquay where I was raised, very creatively in the summer the local churches would charter a boat on a Sunday evening and moor it just off the promenade at high tide. From this there would be music, testimonies and a short sermon. Preaching from a boat has got a good precedent. Knowing how to win people to Christ and desiring to do so was also part of being a Christian and it was being modelled for us continually.

In Aberystwyth my agenda was to grow the church. It's easy to fill a building if you have an attractive enough programme, and I've done it many times that way. But we wanted to make disciples of Jesus Christ. Not just to have people coming inside the building and then going away again, but rather to have people committing their lives to Jesus and then living for him.

The vision crystallized still further one day through a rather disturbing incident. My wife and I were in a local café having coffee together and there was a youngish couple at the table next to us. The man had ordered a filled baguette. When it arrived and the waitress put it on the table in front of him, he caught sight of the size of it. It was quite literally hanging over both sides of the plate. It was truly enormous. He said aloud to the woman who was with him, 'Jesus Christ, will you look at that!' Going back fifty years, that man would not have spoken in that way about Jesus in public. For Jesus Christ to become a commonly accepted swear word marks a huge shift in public behaviour, and it shows a disrespect for the name of our Lord which really is quite shameful. But how could that man recover some respect for Jesus so that in the future he wouldn't speak like that again? Perhaps I should have remonstrated with him in public, but I didn't have the bottle for that.

People have lost respect for Jesus because they have lost respect for his followers and they have lost respect for his church. Is there any way in which that could be recovered? This was my thinking. What if instead of empty buildings being shown on TV we could show to the local community a full building with a thriving congregation? What if instead of our Christians being timid and apologetic, they could be confident and excited? What if instead of our message being presented nervously and falteringly, we could present it rationally and coherently? What if the world could see a community which was operating in love rather than a community of hypocrites? What if? We could then 'recover his reputation'.

'Your name and renown are the desire of our hearts'.[2] There is a deep echo in my soul still as I hear those words from Isaiah. The Lord's reputation means so much, and we have given to the world so many reasons for not respecting him. It is time to reverse that.

Of course, not everyone would agree with 'Recovering His Reputation' as a vision statement. The Normal Distribution Curve is a remarkably accurate way of describing the response of a group of people to something new and different. The curve on the graph is bell shaped. There are those who leap at any new idea and are on board immediately, that's how the graph begins. Then there are those who, with the minimum amount of persuasion, give their agreement to the new idea, so the number of people in support begins to grow quickly. Then there are those who are still persuadable but you're going to have to work harder to get them on

---

[2] Isaiah 26:8.

board. Then at the far end of the curve are those who will not come with you whatever you do.

Whilst there were some who on hearing that 'Recovering His Reputation' was going to be our vision statement were with us from the word 'go', simultaneously there were a few who said, 'But he's never lost his reputation'. That's absolutely true. In heaven he has not lost his reputation, but in the local community of Aberystwyth for some people he has lost his reputation to the extent that the name of Jesus is just an expletive to be used when an oversized baguette is delivered to the table.

Others with similar doubts said, 'You can't use that as your vision statement. It is too obscure. We don't know what you mean by it.' No amount of explanation seemed to sway them. So there were a few who were never at ease with our vision. But most found it entirely captivating and motivating. Some people from away even wanted to borrow it and to use it for their own churches. Perhaps we should have refused and let them find their own way of expressing their vision, but we didn't.

I realise that vision casting by the leader is something very personal and very individual. Frequently a vision will not last beyond the period of the minister who introduces it, but that does not make it invalid nor irrelevant for that time. If the leader is not captivated by the vision, then there is nothing to share with the congregation.

One way or the other we dare not continue with the unwritten vision of many churches, defined by one church leader as 'doing laps.' That's precisely where many Anglican churches are today. The lap begins with Advent Sunday in late November. That's always seen as the beginning of the church's year focusing on the second coming of Christ which is guaranteed by his first coming at Christmas. Then there's a breather before Lent begins leading up to Easter. From Easter we look forward to Pentecost. After that we're into the summer programme. As the autumn begins, we have our Harvest Festivals and then we look forward to Advent and the lap begins again. Some of us would see this as visionless Christianity, a church making no progress, having no direction, except constantly going around in circles.

Without a vision we are simply at the mercy of events. We are responding all the time to the unfolding circumstances of the day. If we are not dominated by a vision which drives us then we'll find ourselves at the mercy of the whims of the most influential people around us, we'll be followers of fashions and fads, and worst of all we will have made no measurable progress.

For ourselves, we wanted to recover his reputation by having more and more people becoming disciples of Christ. That would be good for them and it would silence the sceptics at the same time. We wanted to recover his reputation by presenting the Christian message in a way that was coherent, intelligent, reasonable, accessible and persuasive. We wanted to recover his reputation by seeing people experience the impact of the presence and power of God's Spirit at work in their lives and their circumstances. We wanted to recover his reputation by filling our building with a thriving congregation that would demonstrate the continuing relevance of Jesus in our age. We wanted to recover his reputation by seeing prayers being answered, with bodies, minds and hearts being healed. We wanted to recover his reputation by pursuing excellence in all that we did instead of projecting an image of poverty, with the church as one more beggar on the street trying to scrape together a few more pennies.

If the vision was clear in that we wanted to bring honour to the name of the Lord, then our means of achieving that end also needed to be clear. This then was our agreed mission statement:

> Our aim is growth in the spiritual maturity of all who worship here and numerical growth through the winning of new people to Christ by the efforts of each member of the church.

We recognised that it would be a hopeless enterprise trying to bring people into a dysfunctional congregation, so we had to work continually on the spiritual maturing of our existing membership whilst simultaneously reaching out to those who were outside of our church. We needed to place a high value on our relationships as a Christian family in Aberystwyth, as well as a high value in reaching out to others. We would grow together whilst on the move in the fulfilling of our vision.

The pioneers of the Methodist Forward Movement in South Wales during the Victorian era made phenomenal spiritual and numerical progress. When the second generation of leaders took over they had a watchword for the next stage of the development of their cause – consolidation.[3] That was the very moment when their decline began. Up until that decision they were still growing, but when they turned their energies to consolidating their gains the progress stopped. What a lesson for our church. Consolidation is not an inspiring vision. It doesn't carry with it any sense of adventure or risk. It doesn't invite enterprise, the pushing of boundaries or much creativity. It conveys settling down, protecting what we already have, circling the wagons, being immobile. The 'Forward' movement became the 'Static' movement.

The first objective of our mission statement required a carefully planned teaching programme together with encouraging a strong sense of community and that was to be achieved primarily through developing still further the already existing home groups. The second objective would be achieved through mobilising the congregation to be inviters, to have regular guest events and particularly to gather around the vision of end to end Alpha courses. This was to be a whole church enterprise. It couldn't just be done by the leader alone.

The principles relating to these two objectives and the implications of what they looked like in the overall life of the church were crystalized in a sixteen point document entitled 'Values and

---

[3] For more on this, see Geraint Fielder, *Grace, Grit and Gumption: Spiritual Revival in South Wales* (Fearn: Christian Focus Publications, 2004).

Aspirations'.[4] This was given to the congregation, outlining the expectations that the leadership had of each church member. These principles of our corporate behaviour were to be implemented immediately. Those congregations which plan a year of prayer and then a year of preparation, then a year of teaching, followed by a year of outreach have already lost the plot. Who knows whether the ministry leaders will still be in place in four years time? Maybe the Lord will have returned by then and evangelism will no longer be necessary. No, the time is now. This is for every leader and for every congregation of whatever size. Vision motivates. Money, energy, resources, personnel, flow towards vision. Let's get on with it. Hone the vision. Cast the vision. Implement the vision.

The first paragraph of the 'Foreword' I wrote for our centenary history of St Michael's Aberystwyth in 1990 begins with these words:

> Every church is unique. Not only because of the architecture and furnishings which stamp the individuality of the architect and the character of the local community onto the building, but also because of the unique make-up of the membership of each congregation with their own individual personalities, gifts and characteristics. It is as though each church, the building and the congregation together, is a fingerprint of God upon earth. Different from every other one. Special in its own way.[5]

If only I'd listened to myself more! If we put two congregations side by side and they both have 100 members then logic says that those two churches will be faced by the same problems and will have the same opportunities. What congregation number one can do, congregation number two could also do. The ministers from these two churches should get together and learn from each other. Except that this logic does not work in practice.

---

[4] See chapter entitled 'Values and aspirations'.
[5] See Noel Butler, *You are my Witnesses: St. Michael's, Aberystwyth 1890-1990* (Aberystwyth: Aberart 1990).

Maybe in congregation number one there is a group of people who have a strongly compassionate heart and they begin an outreach programme for the homeless. But if in congregation number two there are no people like that then they may try to start a compassion ministry in imitation of congregation number one, but the people will feel that they neither have the motivation nor the giftedness to do it. If their minister tries to force them to be like the first church then they'll need to be beaten into submission. They will try to fulfil what the minister calls them to do but they will do it reluctantly and badly because they do not have the same gift mix or motivation. They will look at church number one which is thriving and succeeding in that particular ministry area and be made to feel guilty and a failure because they have not done so well.

Our churches are very prone to getting on the latest bandwagons. I saw the red light flashing when at a conference for leaders of larger churches one of the delegates said to me, 'There's not much for us to learn here as we already have a dance group, a banner group and a prayer ministry team etc.' If only I had heeded that warning light sooner. I could have saved our congregation from being Toronto-ed, Willow Creek-ed, Alpha-ed, Cell Group-ed, Good News Down our Street-ed and a whole lot more. I could have saved the congregation from being pressed into someone else's mould. Instead I could have helped them more quickly to become themselves and more effectively recover his reputation.

But we are driven people, driven for success and driven for growth and anything that we see working somewhere else and which seems to have the anointing of God upon it, we tend to feel that we should be doing that too. Yet, it doesn't work like that. Each congregation is unique with its own pool of gifts, volunteers, resources and finance. What will work in one place, will not necessarily work in another, and we need to listen so carefully to the voice of the Lord and do what he calls us to do. That may well mean not doing what everyone else is doing. It may mean leaving aside what some would consider an essential ministry for a local church, but if we have neither the gifts nor the call of God then it is best for us to leave those things alone.

A church which is listening carefully to the voice of the Spirit will be marked out by what it is not doing, as well as by what it is doing. This is such an important principle that I almost want to write it in bold print. At a conference for evangelists our speaker introduced himself with the words, 'I come from the only Alpha-free zone in the UK!' He got the laugh that his joke deserved, but his comment contained a serious truth. His parish was working class. Many members of his congregation had literacy problems. Alpha would have been completely inappropriate for his people. He needed something else which would communicate with them at their level. His parish was marked out by what it was not doing, under the guidance of the Spirit.

If there is no-one truly gifted in children's work in the congregation then no children's work will be happening, and neither should it be. If there's no-one with musical gifts then there'll be no choir or worship band. Even when we do have the gifts, we need to ensure that we are not simply imitating others in their programmes and their style, but rather developing something that is unique to the membership that the Lord has given to us.

In addition to that it is fairly obvious that a church with twenty members cannot do what a church with fifty members is able to do. Instead of aspiring to be what others are, and aspiring to do what others are doing, we need to aspire to be ourselves under the guidance and inspiration of the Spirit. That requires a carefully listening ear and a measure of patience to allow the Lord to show us. This is the very point at which the minister must take the lead ensuring that the whole church is listening sensitively to the voice of the Spirit.

The pressure to implement new schemes and programmes can be considerable, from within ourselves because we long to see progress, but also from ministerial colleagues who hold up their stories of success before our eyes, and even members of our own congregation who long for more and tell us that the secret lies in a particular strategy or blessing. We then feel coerced into implementing some new programme through a kind of spiritual blackmail rather than through the promptings of the Spirit of God.

One of the fascinating features of church life in Aberystwyth was the way that over the years the unique call of God was manifested in the lives of individual congregations in the town. The Elim Pentecostal church had a number of enthusiastic youth leaders and they developed a youth outreach programme. Alfred Place Baptist church founded a ministry to people with learning difficulties as a result of one couple in their congregation having a child with those issues. The Salvation Army set up a furniture re-cycling business called Craft where furniture was repaired and given to needy families or sold. Morfa Chapel built a community and cultural centre called Y Morlan whilst St Anne's church started the Jubilee Storehouse which is a Food Bank for the needy. St Michael's organised Night Light which was a Street Pastor initiative with church members out on the streets on a Friday or Saturday night bringing help to those who had partied too hard. They also still run the Hatch which is a free Sunday lunch for the homeless and disadvantaged.

In fact, when all of these different enterprises are added together we can see the whole vision of God being expressed for the whole town but through the different giftings and passions of individual congregations. Without any one of those congregations and any one of those enterprises then the work of God in Aberystwyth would have been less than the Lord himself desired it to be. As each one listened to the voice of the Lord and followed his leading, they set up different yet complimentary ministries so the heart of God for the town became clearer. One congregation on its own could not achieve the will of God for Aberystwyth, but the sum total of all of those enterprises and all of those church members in all of those different churches succeeded in expressing the heart of God for the whole area.

Each congregation, responding to the call of the Lord, but doing it in different ways according to the vision of their members and their mix of gifts and their varying interests. This is surely the way that it ought to be, but somehow when the pressure is on it's so tempting simply to try to do what others are doing. Yet no two fingerprints are the same, neither are any two congregations the same however similar they may look at first glance. A church in the process of becoming who we are. That seems like a good and right insight to me now!

When a church is built by the Spirit of God rather than the charisma of the minister then there will be one other remarkable feature about it; a complete cross section of the local community will be present and not just one particular demographic. I referred to St Michael's, Aberystwyth as a 'Student Church' on one occasion in my early days there and was reprimanded quickly and rightly by some of the older members who said that that description made them feel excluded and devalued. I never used it again.

Over the years what was remarkable about our congregation was the breadth of people present from right across the social spectrum, from the illiterate to university professors, from farmers and self-employed tradesmen to high flying professionals, from people with mental illness to those who supported them, together with a broad range of ethnic variation representing those who had come to study or to live in the town. There were not many areas of town life which were not represented in our church. In addition to that we took a gender census on one occasion to check the balance of men and women in the congregation. It was a Sunday evening with a little over 200 people present and there were just four more women present than men at that service.

We also had a substantial community of people with learning difficulties coming from two residential homes in the area. They were highly valued members of our congregation and deeply loved. I made one mistake with them when we were invited by the BBC to do a live TV broadcast of a Sunday morning service. Because some of the people with learning difficulties found it hard to sit still for the whole service we asked their carers not to bring them for that particular day. I still feel ashamed of that decision. The church didn't look right without them. It was not representative of our usual congregation. I'll never do that again!

If it is true that each congregation is a unique fingerprint of God in the world, then it is also true that that fingerprint will be constantly changing; there will be some who leave for whatever reason and others who will come. The ebb and flow of a congregation is something which is beyond the control of the leader and they need to be completely relaxed about that, recognising that with the moving on of certain people it may well mean that some ministries within the church have to cease, sometimes temporarily and sometimes permanently. Of course, with that ebb and flow it may well be that new ministries which have been longed for and prayed about may suddenly become possible when new gifted people move into the area or are converted to Christ.

A congregation is never static and for us in Aberystwyth we never ever had the same congregation two Sundays running, between the students during term time and the tourists in the summer there was a constantly changing tapestry of people inside the building. That was one of the many glories of the place.

One of the other very special features of St Michael's was the worship group which had been established by Bertie Lewis. He was himself extremely gifted musically but he had an idea about blending the traditional and the modern which made the church almost unique. The membership of the worship group was drawn out of the choir. This meant that everyone who sang or played in church was committed to the whole worship life of the church and not just to the part which could so easily have had the greater prominence and kudos. In addition to that it gave the members of the worship group the opportunity to listen to the newer members of the choir and to select out those who had voices which would blend with the overall musical style of the group.

Not only were the worship group and the choir all one body without tension or competition between them, but there was also a commitment to retain traditional hymn singing as well as to develop an increasing repertoire of contemporary Christian songs, some of them written in house. That blend of modern and traditional made St Michael's into a wonderful place to worship and frequently services were quite heavenly in the way that we were drawn close to the Lord. Both traditions were honoured, neither one was displaced by the other. All generations were served by such an approach and we were able to select out the best of the best in terms of choosing music, hymns and songs which inspired the heart and motivated the soul. Often there was only one word to describe the worship in our church; beautiful.

Because we had such good quality musical leadership the BBC came back to us again and again to broadcast on Radio 4. One of our early broadcasts produced a special postal delivery of over 800 letters. That kind of response led subsequently to a number of TV broadcast Sunday services which went out live. Again, thrilling opportunities to speak to the nation about Christ.

The fingerprints of God in St Michael's Aberystwyth included those particularly gifted musicians at that particular time. Those fingerprints were so distinctive that when our students graduated and moved away we would tell them repeatedly, 'You will never find another St Michael's anywhere.' That was not intended to be a boast, but was a simple reality. This church was unique because of the people who belonged to it and the gifts which they contributed to it. That statement should be and could be made about any and every church congregation. Every single church is unique. Let's help it to be itself still more fully. We need to celebrate that distinctiveness rather than constantly wish that it was different in some way. Whether there are five people in attendance or fifty or 500, the challenge to the church is the same, and the role of helping a congregation to become itself would take a lot of stress out of the life of every minister. It's much easier than trying to become someone else and it is all part and parcel of recovering his reputation.

Thinking moment

- What is the vision for your local church? Can you quote it by heart? Are you supporting that vision or do you think that it needs to be revisited, even re-written?

- Is your congregation really different from any other that you know? How would you describe in a few words its unique character?

Making disciples

'Instruct the wise and they will be wiser still; teach the righteous and they will add to their learning' (Proverbs 9:9).

'Renovating buildings is much easier than renovating people', commented Bishop John Richards to me on one occasion. He was right. Straighten the spire, re-order the interior, install a good sound system, a coat or two of paint and a new carpet and the job's done. When ministers renovate a building they have something to show for their ministry; something that they can go back and look at; something that stays in one place. That's why they spend so much time doing it. But people matter so much more than the buildings. It's just that renovating people is such an unpredictable process that it will take a lifetime and can only truly start once a person has become a disciple of Jesus.

This is an area in which our congregations need to be challenged. Do they consider themselves to be believers, to be attenders, to be worshippers, to be Christians or to be disciples? To believe is something that we do in the mind whilst our bodies may be absent. To attend is something that we do with our bodies whilst our minds may be absent. To be worshippers is something that we do with our voices but again our minds may be absent. To be Christians is just a title we choose to use for ourselves, but it may have little impact on our behaviour. But to be a disciple, now that really does tie us down. It describes a personal link between the individual and the Lord.

To be a disciple means that we are following someone. To be a disciple means that we are listening to their teaching and seeking to put it into practice. To be a disciple means that we will be modelling ourselves after the teacher. To be a disciple means that we will be receiving instruction, and submitting ourselves to it. To be a disciple means that we want to be taught, to learn, to have ignorance dispelled even to unlearn bad habits and thought patterns from the past.

We are living through an era when many people are haunted by an identity crisis. They don't know who they are and are trying to clarify things in their own mind by appealing to their ethnicity, their skin colour, their political views, their sexual preferences, their cultural background. Young people are taking so long to grow up and to find themselves. The primary reason for this lack of identity is an empty soul. God 'has set eternity in the human heart'.[1] This is not just a theological statement but also a psychological reality. When I solidified my commitment to Christ at the age of seventeen my identity was fixed. I was and remain entirely secure. I am a disciple of Jesus.

I have found over the years that the description of myself as a disciple of Jesus Christ has silenced opposition and argument and created a new atmosphere for discussion with people. When challenged on how I could possibly hold this view or that view, I have replied, 'I think like this because I am a disciple of Jesus Christ.' In other words, if you want to argue with me you're going to have to argue with him because all I'm saying is what he said. I'm reflecting back to you what he taught. That is a great defence. Taking on Jesus is a bigger challenge than taking on me.

Whilst in Aberystwyth we wanted to see people converted, but more than anything else we wanted to see them become disciples of Jesus. So in order to nurture disciples we had a multi-disciplinary approach. There was not just one method which we embraced but a series of different methods on offer simultaneously.

Our primary discipleship programme was through the ministry of preaching and teaching on a Sunday.[2] The intention of each sermon was to instruct, to inform, to challenge, to inspire and to direct the lives of those who were listening. We were intentionally practical and motivational, just as Jesus was himself. If people came to church regularly and gave serious attention to the sermons,

---

[1] Ecclesiastes 3:11.
[2] See chapter entitled 'Out of the pulpit'.

then they would go home with enough information to know how to live the Christian life effectively.

Alongside the Sunday preaching was the instruction given in the setting of mid-week home groups. There were already half a dozen when I arrived in the parish in 1988 and this was an area of ministry we were keen to develop. Pastor David Yonggi Cho from Seoul, South Korea became something of a Christian celebrity towards the end of the twentieth century. He had established the largest church in the world with a membership of one and a quarter million. His Yoido Full Gospel Church building seated 12,000 people and there were seven services every Sunday with the next congregation queuing up outside as the previous one left. Not only were there overflow meetings but also other satellite congregations around the city. For all of his faults, and by all accounts there were many, Yonggi Cho was an organisational genius.

His method for discipling his members, holding on to them, teaching them the faith and keeping contact with them was the Cell Group. He made the claim that he was only four people away from any one member of his congregation. The way that he had organised them was to provide a leader for the group, but then he provided a leader for every fifty leaders in order to look after them, and then leaders for those leaders who were then in turn answerable to him. As a system of organisation it had a huge amount to commend it. With this as a model there was no limit to the expansion of the church. It was an organism not an organisation.

He had two other principles linked to the groups. His ideal was for them to be as local as possible so that people didn't have to travel too far to attend the weekly meetings and that they would provide friendship, support and encouragement to each other as well as evangelise in their localities. Secondly, he commended the concept of homogeneous groups so that for example medics would get together or people in the legal profession would form a group and so on. That way, not only did they have their faith in common, but as they were faced by the same issues at work day by day they could help one another in applying their faith to their daily circumstances.

During the autumn of 1997 my wife and I were encouraged by our own church leadership to attend the 16th Annual Church Growth International conference in Seoul. The Sunday services in the Yoido Full Gospel church were a revelation with exuberant singing, the extraordinary experience of 'Korean praying' (everyone praying aloud from the heart together at the same time until a little bell was rung to finish the intercessions), simultaneous translation of the sermon into multiple languages, and communion for 12,000 people which took less than ten minutes.

All of his teaching about Cell Groups made sense to me, but when applied in a wooden way in Aberystwyth there were pitfalls which I had not foreseen in our very different context. On our return from Korea Rehoboam's young advisers said, 'Go for it straight away. Let's implement these principles and make the necessary changes in the St Michael's congregation.' Solomon's advisers said, 'Take your time. There's no hurry. Give this some more thought.'

I didn't listen to my younger advisers, but neither did I listen well enough to my older advisers. Sooner than I should have done I tried to implement a policy of making our home groups local. I divided them up in a different way in order to stop people from criss-crossing the town. But inadvertently I disturbed some relationships and friendships which had developed over several years. Some of the group members were lost as a result of that, and others took years to heal and to re-identify with another group. A policy might work on paper, but people don't live their lives on paper, they live them in the real world.

And what about homogeneous groups? There is an argument which is as strongly against them as in favour of them. I found Yonggi Cho convincing in his reasoning that a group of people from the same profession can understand each other well and help each other in applying their Christian faith to their daily work.

However, how much more like the kingdom of God does a group appear when it is made up of a complete cross section of people of different ages, backgrounds, education, and ethnicity? To me that is what the kingdom of God looks like. To me this is something that cannot be found in the secular world. That's where patience is required and love and gentleness, and a whole lot more. This is the environment in which we can truly grow and care for each other. It is really hard work and requires much more grace than being in a room with people we like and with whom we can identify easily.

Nonetheless, despite all of the problems and all of the mistakes I am convinced that the small group life of the church is by far the best place for spiritual growth, for building community and for the discipling of the congregation. It is significant that the 3000 who became believers on the day of Pentecost organised themselves (or were organised by the apostles) into house fellowships. That surely is the implication of what we read in the Acts of the Apostles, 'They broke bread in their homes and ate together with glad and sincere hearts'.[3]

At the height of our numerical growth in 2002 and 2003, we had over 400 people in 38 different groups. In order to cope with those numbers we had to implement a system of 'bishops' to look after the group leaders. Their task was to mentor the leaders under their care, to meet with them regularly, to encourage them, and to advise them when there were difficulties. Those 'bishops' met with me several times a term for lunch and during that session we would receive reports on each group, their strengths and weaknesses, their successes and their failures. This was the way that we provided pastoral care for the congregation.

However, this was only about 60% of our attending worshippers. In every church there will be those for whom their season of life would keep them away from a home group, either they were raising a young family or had demanding work responsibilities or had become frail and elderly, and then there are always those who are

[3] Acts 2:46.

so shy and introverted that being part of such a group would be crucifying. Our database contained over 750 names of people who were part of our church family. Keeping track of everyone was a major task and required as much organisation as anything else. We developed our own pastoral care team and at the beginning of each week we would try to keep an eye on who had been present at worship, who had missed and why. It was absolutely vital that we tracked people's attendance as much as we possibly could in order to keep in touch with them and their circumstances.

The keeping of any kind of register would definitely be prohibited these days because of all the restrictions over data protection. However, any pastor worthy of the name will be looking for some creative ways to ensure that they are tracking the attendance of their people. Almost invariably I have found that members of our congregations have liked to be missed and have liked it to be noticed when they don't turn up. It is a sign that they belong and that they are important to the rest of us. When I have followed up on someone's absence from worship, I have almost never had a negative or aggressive response. Jesus portrays himself as the one who goes out after the sheep which didn't come home.[4] How much more is it the responsibility of the minister and others who are appointed into pastoral leadership to do the same?

One of the lessons that I was very slow to learn was the value of tying the home group material into the teaching life of the church so that the whole congregation could move forward together. For nearly twenty years I had missed this. We had a Sunday morning teaching series moving through something from the Old Testament, then something from the New Testament, and then a topical series. On a Sunday evening we had a freer preaching programme, sometimes themed and sometimes not. Then in the home groups we would have a third study programme. When I finally woke up to the foolishness of this, we tied the Sunday morning series (because this was the largest congregation) into the home group study material, and that was when almost the whole

---

[4] Luke 15:4.

church began to move forward together. It made an immense amount of difference. Now instead of 60% of the congregation receiving the same teaching we had closer to 100% who were doing so. It gave a much more united feel to the church's life and to the sense of growing together in knowledge, understanding and grasp of the faith.

Whilst I had no problem at all about using 'pre-packaged' material which had been produced by other churches I was at pains to ensure that we didn't use that material in an inflexible way. Quite often material would come with its own discussion questions for group work and frequently those questions would bear little relationship to the needs of our parish and the life experience of our members. Almost always the material needed to be adapted and made appropriate for our own people.

I felt that it was my responsibility to hold the reins of the home groups, the material that we studied, the way that it was angled, and the application of the subjects. If as the leader of the church I was to set the agenda, vision and destination of the church then I needed to hold on to this area of ministry and not delegate it to another. This was too important an aspect of our church's life to hand on to someone else, however gifted they might have been.

One other amusing and interesting sidelight on the whole issue of home groups was that it didn't matter what the material was that we were going to follow, there was always one group that didn't like it, and it wasn't the same group every time. It seemed as though the torch of objection was handed on to a different group. So when we watched some Rick Warren material, from Saddleback Community Church in California there were some who didn't like his Hawaiian shirts. When we used *Knowing God* by Jim Packer there were some who thought that was too impenetrable to follow, and so it went on. In fact, each time there was a new launch we were watching and waiting to find which group didn't like it, and there was always one!

At the heart of any growing church there must be community. Home groups or something similar are essential to the development of that community life. In their informality, their flexibility and their developing intimacy they provide the backbone of the life of the church. They are hard work and demanding, but they make all the difference between having an assembly of individual Christians and the creation of a family of believers.

I appreciate that our experience of home groups cannot be echoed in some other communities because of the local culture where people are unfamiliar with inviting their friends to their home. This is particularly true in a rural context. However, there are a number of ways to begin to overcome those obstacles by starting in the minister's own home so that people can get a feel for what such a meeting would look like.[5] As a result they might not feel so threatened when asked if they would be willing to host something similar in their own homes. If local homes are unavailable then a room in the church or village hall or school would do to begin with. Anything we can do to create intimacy, openness and a sense of a Christian family is to be encouraged.

The home group programme was backed up by a system of one to one mentoring for those who elected to receive it. This allowed some greater in-depth exploration of the spiritual development of the individual and meant that greater progress could be made more quickly. There was a reasonably formal agreement with the person being discipled. Our expectations were not too demanding but included a request that the person would be committed to growing as a disciple, that they would be honest, that they would turn up to appointments, that they would be willing to resolve conflicts if they arose and that the whole process would be bathed in prayer.

It was entirely confidential, but it was intentional and searching just the same. We wanted to walk the tightrope between being directive and non-directive; recognising that we did not have the right or the authority to tell people what to do, but nonetheless we were more

---

[5] See chapter entitled 'Into retirement'.

than a shoulder to cry on. We did want to help people make progress with their problems and temptations and also to grow in their walk with God.

There was a group of trusted and mature Christian leaders who took on these responsibilities. It was highly valued by all who participated and we never had any problems relating either to the process or to those who were involved. In the light of the potential for abuse and the regrettable scandals which have come to light regarding this kind of activity in recent times it is all the more important for there to be proper safeguarding training and careful supervision. But as a means of progressing the development of serious discipleship it has much to commend it.

It became clear to us that given more time we could make still more progress more rapidly. As a result, we established the Aberystwyth Academy of Christian Discipleship in 2002. There is a long and distinguished history of academies in Wales. Before the opportunities which universal education presented there were academies set up in barns and cow sheds by the nonconformists for training their own ministers. These were small local initiatives. We chose the title of Academy because of this association with the Christian history of Wales. Our plan was to train people full time in Wales for Wales, although that was not an exclusive vision.
The whole enterprise was supported by all of the churches of the town, so it was interdenominational in ethos and we made use of the specialist expertise of members of other congregations as well as our own to provide the teaching. There were other lecturers too who travelled longer distances to give their time because they shared our vision.

We were aware that Christians need to know their Bibles and often don't. We knew too that Christians need to have a practical grasp of Christian doctrine so they would know what to say when someone raised questions about the faith or had a wayward child, a non-Christian partner, a bereavement in the family, wanted an abortion, had marital problems, and so much more. We also thought it would be a help to know how the church has got to be the way that it is so that we could try to avoid re-making the mistakes of the past.

Alongside the teaching side of the course we wanted our people to have the opportunity to gain practical experience in various aspects of Christian work. Our plan was to give training on the job in an apprenticeship-style course. We could expose our participants to ministry in just about every conceivable setting apart from heavy industry as that is largely absent in west Wales.

The course began with an outward-bound component which was something of a challenge for our more mature students. A three-day spiritual retreat was included as well as a church-based mission somewhere in Wales. A typical week comprised two days in the classroom, two days of practical work somewhere in the church or in the community and one study day. During the whole year each one of our students was provided with the same one-to-one mentoring for their own personal development.

When we began we were accredited by Bangor University at certificate level. There were six full-time students for four years in a row. One of the highest accolades from one of our students was that he had learned more in one year on the Academy course than he had done in three years at theological college!

When there were insufficient candidates to support a full-time course we took a break but then reformed the Academy under the title, Fast Forward, by offering individual modules covering similar themes. That again lasted for a further four years. Once again, we took a break and then launched a new programme of monthly Saturday Schools under the title of Momentwm. This was a whole day of classroom-based work with two sessions in the morning and two in the afternoon. Again we were committed to covering the contents of the Bible, some doctrinal reflections, and some attention to church history before concluding the day with a session on some area of practical Christian ministry. This again lasted for a further four years.

We read that 'Jesus grew in wisdom and stature and in favour with God and man.'[6] If anyone wanted to grow in St Michael's, Aberystwyth, then there were plenty of ways in which they could do so. Making disciples was not something left to chance.

Thinking moment

- Who was the key person who influenced your spiritual growth? Have you ever told them how important they were to your spiritual development? Who are you helping to grow spiritually in your turn?

- What was the most important factor for you in your discipleship? Was it the influence of a person, a small group, a book, a sermon, a conference, some spiritual encounter? What are you doing currently to stimulate further development in your Christian life?

---

[6] Luke 2:52.

Permission refusers

'Whatever your hand finds to do, do it with all your might' (Ecclesiastes 9:10)

The young man had moved to Aberystwyth to continue his academic career in post- doctoral research. He was an enthusiastic Christian and was sitting in my study explaining his proposal to try to get together people like himself who would be keen to read the Bible. He wanted that enterprise to be used as a means for some further evangelistic outreach into the university.

Having heard his proposal I outlined to him what our policy was regarding home groups and Bible study. We were working hard to integrate all of the students into our existing system so that they were evenly spread among our other church members. This meant that the students were not gathered together into a little clique of their own, and they would have their feet firmly on the ground as they shared their lives with a cross section of people from different age groups and backgrounds; town and gown were mixed up together. That was our policy. So I tried to dissuade this young man from his proposal. At the conclusion of our conversation he rather wistfully said, 'I've never before been discouraged by a minister from studying the Bible with other people'. My apologies to you, Richard.

Some leaders like to be permission refusers. I suppose it gives them a sense of being in control, of making the tough decisions and of ensuring that there is order rather than chaos in their church's programme. But the more inflexibly we implement our vision the more discouraged our people will become. That young man didn't leave my study envisioned and enthused but put down and disheartened.

'Anyone can do anything in our church so long as it doesn't require profile, or finance or staff time', said a delegate at the Larger

Churches Conference I was attending. 'So long as we don't have to push the enterprise from the front of church. So long as we don't have to put our hands into the church's financial resources. So long as this proposal doesn't require the involvement of one or more of our church staff. Then get on with it.'

The result of adopting that as a policy for us was a multiplication of ministries of all kinds which developed out of the energies, gifts and commitment of so many others. A substantial proportion of these ministries were not my idea nor were they driven from the top. They came into being through the enterprise of others. Yet all of them together contributed to our over-arching vision of Recovering His Reputation.

One of the reasons that some leaders are permission refusers is that they don't want anyone else in their circle to have any of the glory. So they hold tightly to the reins of leadership and micromanage every area of church life. No church can grow with that as a policy. Looking back, in almost every case, it is possible to remember the person who brought forward the idea for various ministries in St Michael's, and even the occasion when it happened. We need to surround ourselves with the go-getters, the creatives, the ideas people and give them their head. Having given them their head we need to give them our encouragement, support, and most particularly the praise and the applause when things go right. There's nothing to fear from letting others be the initiators of new things. Everyone wins.

Nightlight was a very successful street pastor scheme which was launched by a young couple in St Michael's. They had heard about what was happening in other major towns and cities across the country and offered to take the lead in initiating and running a similar enterprise in Aberystwyth. When they first brought this idea to me, I could have immediately given a number of reasons why it shouldn't happen. I could have said that we would be competing for volunteers. It would absorb some of the giving in the church and divert it into another enterprise. It would be time consuming and draining for those who had participated, lessening their involvement in other parts of church life. Rehoboam would have said to himself 'Don't let go of the reins of control' and would have said to the young couple, 'No. Permission refused.' Solomon would have said, 'Yes. Permission given. If it is of the Lord then it will succeed, and if it isn't then no harm has been done.'

Within just a few weeks they had recruited an interdenominational team of over forty people, trained them, set up the necessary insurances, purchased the equipment and were going out into the town on a Friday or Saturday night from 11 pm until 3 am to be involved in the support of young people who had had too much to drink. In no time at all they had the enthusiastic support of the local police force and there was a great deal of reported appreciation for what they were doing from the publicans and bouncers as well. This was a ministry which lasted for nearly a decade and was handed on to a succession of equally committed leaders.

It didn't conflict with anything else that we were already doing. It was not a competitive enterprise draining the life out of other ministries but rather the reverse, it was contributing to the overall vision and was energising to those who were involved in it giving a wonderful outlet to their Christian commitment. In addition to that the local community saw a church which was practically involved in the life of the town. This was 'Recovering His Reputation' on the streets of the town.

One of the inherent dangers of a ministry which begins through the enthusiasm and energy of a particular visionary is the succession of leadership when that person moves on. If there is no-one with the same mix of gifts stepping into the leadership role then the temptation is for the ministry to land on the desk of the senior leader. That is the worst case scenario and must never be allowed to happen.

The next worst is for it to be absorbed into the overall programme of the church, and then what began as a volunteer led ministry becomes one which requires all the things that it didn't need when it began – profile from the front to push it along, a budget from church finances and a member of staff to take on the supervision and recruiting of volunteers.

Sometimes that may be the right thing to do, but more often than not the bolder option and more faith filled option is to allow the ministry to die or go into cold storage unless and until a new volunteer leader steps forward. If the gifted volunteers are not in place, then surely that particular ministry cannot be the Lord's will for the current time. We allow ourselves to get stressed too much when we see a gap opening up in various leadership roles, when we should be more courageous and confident in recognising the signs that a ministry should be terminated, either temporarily or permanently. We need to have enough trust in the Lord that if he hasn't provided the necessary leaders or finance or resources then it's time for that particular enterprise to close.

We have all heard of the leader who refuses permission for a particular initiative but when six months or so have passed comes up with the idea themselves. We also know the exhausting kind of leader who comes up with a dozen new ideas before breakfast and then wears everyone out either trying to implement them or trying to discern which if any is the best. The truth is that it doesn't matter who brings forward any suggestion, what matters is whether or not it is a proposal which has come from the Lord himself. Sometimes, unfortunately, it is only possible to discern that in retrospect. Has the enterprise flourished and has the hand of heaven been upon it or has it simply died in the gestation period?

The children's and youth ministries in St Michael's were not only well resourced with full time salaried leaders but they were themselves the initiators of hugely successful spin off ministries. Close to fifty years ago there was a beach mission running every summer in the coastal village of Borth some five miles to the north of Aberystwyth. That had long since finished but in 2004 there was now new enthusiasm for maximising the opportunities of running something similar in Aberystwyth. The Band Stand on the promenade was a superb public facility and has been used for many years attracting large numbers of local children as well as youngsters coming to the town on holiday.

Perhaps the best of all the initiatives which emerged from the children's ministry was our annual Stable Trail retelling the events of the first Christmas through dramatic presentations on a Saturday early in December. It has had a substantial impact on the town. The record for attendance is still going up and is currently around the 400 mark for children alone, excluding their parents, grandparents and other family members. Just imagine that. 400 families talking about the Christmas events. 400 or more parents. 400 homes. 400 school children talking about it during break time at school on the following Monday morning. How good is that?

This outreach involved transforming the church building over a period of a couple of days creating different rooms where scenes from the Christmas events are portrayed. The whole tour which is accompanied by one of the Sunday Club leaders comes to a climax in the cave stable often with a live baby. The baby will never remember their part in the proceedings, but its parents will never forget it. The day you were Jesus! These are the things that memories are made of, and the impact of it on the town is substantial.

Some church leaders find themselves threatened when other gifted leaders join their congregation and try to keep them at arm's length (unbelievably, sometimes even asking them to go elsewhere). One very erudite and well-read Methodist minister retired to Aberystwyth and came to St Michael's. He was a man who seemed to have read all of the mainstream theologians and many, many more besides. He was well able to speak authoritatively on past and present theological fashions, and could summarise the positions and theories of many of the Christian writers and church leaders. He is experienced in theological education and wanted to offer a series of sessions for those who wished to explore some of the deeper issues of the faith. This is the moment when the leader finds out what they are made of. It would have been so easy to refuse his request and with plenty of good reasons. I could have argued that we already have a full programme of Christian discipleship in the life of the church. It is carefully structured. There's no room for anything in addition to what we are already doing. This will create confusion in the minds of the congregation. They won't know which session to choose. I can hear all of the reasons against his proposals still going around in my head, although none of them were ever verbalised. (What if this new man turned out to be a better teacher than me, and people preferred it when he was speaking? Shhhhh! Don't let anyone think that such an idea could cross your mind!) Would this man leave my study wistfully saying to himself, 'No-one has ever said that I shouldn't teach the faith in all of its depth and complexity?' In fact, what did happen was that those evening sessions by such an erudite theologian took place and were enormously valued by a substantial number of people over a period of several years.

Another retired FIEC minister joined us with a lovely gracious and humorous teaching gift. He taught a mid-week series on the outline of the contents of all of the books of the Bible, and subsequently became a regular preacher in the Sunday services and a much valued teacher in our Aberystwyth Academy of Christian Discipleship.

Similarly, one of our church wardens was especially helped by the writings of Dallas Willard, the American Christian philosopher and academic. He had read much of Willard's writings and they had an enormous impact on his own spiritual development.[1] He was so enthused by the changes that it had brought about in his own Christian life that he wanted to run a Delta course. We already had an Alpha course and a Beta course, so why shouldn't there be a Delta course about the writings of 'D' for Dallas; all of it clearly

---

[1] Among these books were Dallas Willard, *The Spirit of the Disciplines: Understanding how God Changes Lives* (1998), and *The Divine Conspiracy: Rediscovering our Hidden Lives in God* (1998).

practical Biblical discipleship material? Again, this was a winner for the church and ran for session after session.

Yet another couple own a smallholding on the edge of town and they wanted their facilities to be used for the Lord. They are committed to ecological farming practices and to encouraging the wildlife (particularly the birds) on their land. Offering monthly meetings for twelve to fifteen people on a Saturday continues to be a feature of their rhythm of life.

Permission refusers stifle innovation and initiative. They close down the ministries of others so that their own ministry may reign supreme. The result? An immobilised congregation whose only responsibilities are to sit up, listen up and pay up. This is a lose/lose environment for everyone, minister and people together.

If Jesus had got some harsh things to say about the servant who buried his talent in the ground[2] then what on earth will he have to say to the minister who buries the gifts of the congregation instead of developing them, encouraging them, releasing them. 'Dig them up', Jesus might say, 'let's get some return on them. Be a permission giver.'

Thinking moment

- Doesn't a leader have to keep a fairly tight rein on the church otherwise there will be chaos with everyone trying to do their own thing?

- Isn't it particularly important in a smaller church for everyone to be committed to a small number of enterprises in order not to dilute the energies, resources and finance of the congregation?

---

[2] Matthew 25:24-30.

Values and aspirations

'Let your eyes look straight ahead, fix your gaze directly before you' (Proverbs 4:25)

Some years ago, I heard of an Anglican congregation where the church leader wanted to get all of his home group leaders together. He was somewhat disappointed and surprised when the turnout at the meeting was less than half of those who had responsibility for running the groups in his church. He was conscious of a malaise in the congregation which had led to a falling off in commitment to the overall life of the church. His response was to suspend all of the groups including the worship group. Their Sunday services were accompanied by a piano only and everyone for some months was invited to consider what it meant to be a Christian disciple and particularly what it would look like to be a member of their church.

In order to help his people work out what commitment to the life of the church would mean he produced several sides of A4 which he presented to them for consideration. It was a series of values which he wanted them to agree to. If they were not acceptable then they were free to move to another church and find one which had a different level of expectation of their members.

This is an unfamiliar idea for us in the Anglican tradition because we are committed to being a church which provides for everyone in our community and we tend to welcome all comers often requiring very little of them, if anything at all. Many other churches in the Nonconformist and House Church streams have a formal statement which establishes from the outset what is required of someone who is accepted into membership. That way everyone knows where they stand.

It took me a long time to recognise how important it is for people to know what is expected of them, both as a Christian but also as a member of their local congregation. If we never tell them then they will never know, and the leaders will suffer from a strange disappointment. It is the disappointment of the congregation not living up to the mark, but no-one has told them what the mark is, so how can they live up to it and how can we be disappointed? But as ministers we are, often! How perverse we can be!

Every congregation has already got a set of values even though they may not be printed on paper. Those values and that particular church culture is an expression of the combination of personalities, gifts and attitudes of all of the members put together. It is also to some degree a reflection of the spiritual maturity of the membership, how much of their past life they have brought with them, how far they have come on the pathway of sanctification, and to some extent also a reflection of the culture of the surrounding community from which they come which has been unconsciously absorbed into the life of the church. It doesn't take many months of worshipping with the same people before it would be possible to write down a list of the values of that congregation, values which they have unconsciously absorbed and which they express week by week in their corporate church life. But this is the important point, it is within our power to mould those values and that culture and to Christianise it for the honour of the Lord and for the good of all.

Jerry Cook was an American pastor who described a church in Washington State that grew in fourteen years to more than 4000 people. He records a commitment that the people at the church made to each other. It says:

> You'll never suffer at my hands. I'll never knowingly say or do anything to hurt you. I'll always, in every circumstance, seek to help and support you. If you're down and I can lift you, I'll do that. If you need something and I have it, I'll share it with you. If I need to, I'll give it to you. No matter what I find out about you, no matter what happens in the future – either good or bad –

my commitment to you will never change. And there's nothing you can do about it![1]

That's the kind of church 4000 people wanted to join. The leadership wanted to mould the congregation into loving one another practically. What an aspiration! What a value!

The leadership in St Michael's produced a list of values and aspirations that we promoted amongst our congregation. We decided to call them 'values and aspirations' so that people would not be discouraged if they felt that for some reason they weren't yet living up to what we were suggesting, but we also wanted them to realise that there was something more for them to reach towards in their own spiritual development. We had a list of sixteen points which centred on a number of key issues.

A culture of love
We would regularly and frequently speak of the 'family' of St Michael's for that was what we had become. It was a statement of the reality of the friendships and the caring ethos that existed between members of the fellowship. No one was excluded. This is the nature of the church biblically. We are children of the one Father. We are spiritual brothers and sisters to each other. For some, the spiritual family that they have in the church is closer than their blood family because of the depth at which they are able to share spiritual things with one another. The Biblical 'theory' needs to be made real in practice by the way that we relate to one another.[2]

However, it's when the congregation itself begins to identify itself as a family that it becomes the most real. When they are choosing that word to describe themselves and their relationships then there

---

[1] Jerry Cook with Stanley C. Baldwin, *Love, Acceptance and Forgiveness: Equipping the Church to be Truly Christian in a Non-Christian World* (Ventura, CA: Regal, 1979), p. 11.
[2] See more on this in chapter entitled 'Stopping the revolving door syndrome'.

has been real progress. Both the apostles Paul and Peter speak about 'God's household'.[3] In St Michael's Aberystwyth we had become that household and we wished to continue to nurture such an outlook and foster it for the future.

One of the issues we faced, like many churches, was that we had a substantial number of people from broken backgrounds and others with mental health issues. Someone once cheekily commented, 'Do you have anyone normal in your congregation?' They could be enormously demanding at times, seeking attention, draining the love tanks of the congregation, being intrusive on the worship by their behaviour, and as they often didn't know how to hold relationships together, they could easily create chaos around them within just a few minutes. We needed to exercise patience with all as they matured in their faith and grew in grace. There is a fabulous comment from Dr A. Rendle Short which has been a compass for me over the years:

> During the great Decian persecution (250 AD) the Church in Rome had under its care a great crowd of widows, orphans, blind, lame and sick folk. The heathen prefect broke into the Church and demanded that the congregation should hand over its treasures to the state. Laurentius the deacon pointed at the crowd of poor and sick and maimed and lonely and said: 'These are the treasures of the Church'.[4]

Here is a guiding principle and a godly value for any congregation.

This 'treasuring' of people must extend to an open hearted and genuine welcome to all. A major blessing in St Michael's was a welcome team which had been formed at the initiative of one of our church members. New people were regularly recruited to the team and it functioned in the morning and the evening both before and after the service. Members of the team were constantly on the lookout for visitors, newcomers and those who had no-one to talk

---

[3] 1 Timothy 3:15 and 1 Peter 4:17.
[4] Quoted in *Every Day with William Barclay* (Alresford: Arthur James Ltd, 1983), p. 176.

to. They were super committed and super efficient. They met before each service for prayer and encouragement.

The danger of such a well-run ministry was that our established members might rely upon them to carry the load of welcoming newcomers and think that they could forget about that as a responsibility which actually belongs to us all. Subsequently, I have heard of a church implementing a 'three-minute rule' which is that everyone in the congregation speaks to someone that they don't know for at least the first three minutes after every service. What a fantastic idea. It would have been in our list of values if I had heard about it in time to implement it.

A culture of a personal devotional life
At the heart of all spiritual maturity is learning to feed one's own soul. The development of a daily discipline and rhythm of life including time alone with the Lord and the Scriptures was given a consistently high profile. Guidance was given in how to structure such a time and how to maintain it despite the pressures of life. It was always recognised that for some depending on their season of life this would be more difficult to maintain, especially for parents with young children and those who might have long working days. Nonetheless it remained an aspiration for all to work towards as their circumstances allowed.

On one occasion I was asked to identify the book which had contributed most to my own spiritual development. I'm sure that I was expected to reply by naming some heavy theological tome, but the truth is that *Ordering your Private World*[5] by Gordon MacDonald was perhaps the book which influenced me the most. In his opening chapter he speaks about the geological phenomenon of sink holes, where underground water courses have washed away the sub soil, and then there is a sudden and unexpected collapse of the surface. Out of this brilliant illustration MacDonald makes the point that we need to ensure that the subsoil of the soul has not

---
[5] Gordon MacDonald, *Ordering your Private World* (Crowborough: Highland, 1987), p. 11

been washed away through our neglect of personal daily time with the Lord. Initially it doesn't show when we neglect our devotional discipline for a while, but it will inevitably lead to spiritual collapse in the long run.

A culture of participation
We would frequently remind the congregation of this 'value' at the beginning of the service, particularly if the first hymn or response or the early part of the service had sounded sluggish and rather listless. From time to time we would stop the service, pause for prayer, call ourselves to attention and focus, and then restart the service.

Strangely enough we always noticed that it had to be emphasised on the Sunday when the clock had changed. It didn't matter whether the hour had gone forwards or backwards, it still seemed to de-stabilise the congregation. We faced a similar problem during stormy weather because the St Michael's building is the first thing that greets a storm from the Irish Sea when it reaches landfall.

Under the leadership of Bertie Lewis the congregation at St Michael's had developed a strong tradition of attending church twice on a Sunday, both morning and evening. The evening was not a re-run of the morning with the same sermon but was usually completely different both in style and content. To get the full value from the life of the church it was beneficial to come twice a Sunday.

This was a 'value' that we wanted to reinforce constantly. If we are to obey the fourth commandment and keep the Sabbath day holy, then we are going to need to give more than an hour and a bit of the day to the Lord. When God finished the work of creation he didn't rest for part of the morning or part of the evening. He rested for the whole day and hallowed the whole day. So we're going to have in mind the giving of the entire day to him for our own spiritual benefit.

The principle of the Sabbath must be one of the most widely disregarded commandments out of the ten, even in churches which boast an enthusiastic spiritual life and seek to teach and obey the Bible in its fullness.

A culture of serving
The Pareto Principle says that 80% of the work is done by 20% of the people. At one stage this was quoted to St Michael's as a comment on the involvement of our church members in the life of the church, suggesting that they were not as committed as they should be. However, when we looked more closely we discovered that for us this was an unhelpful distortion of the truth.

Quite naturally, as in every church, there were some people who were deeply involved and would come to everything that was on. But when we took stock of the gifts being released in the life of the church in one form or another, we could see that some 60% of our worshipping congregation was serving in the church in one way or another. We did some research and had a total of 389 'jobs' to be done in the life of the church and discovered that there were 213 different people who were involved in those particular ministries, substantially more than 20% of our congregation.

One of the gifts of the Alpha course has been to release far more people into the work of evangelism than was seen as being possible before. Previously if someone did not feel that they had any gift for leading another person to Christ, then however laudable and right evangelism might seem they felt that they were off the hook and could devote their energies to some other area of service in the church.

But with Alpha, not only are there those who invite their friends to come, but then a whole team of extra people are needed to lead a discussion, to host tables, to prepare food, to set up the room, to provide the technical support, to distribute fliers, to intercede for the course when it happens and so on. Evangelism becomes a corporate whole church enterprise rather than just the interest of a few specialists.

None is excluded from participation in the work of evangelism and none is excused from it either. This is the work of the church and the privilege of all contributing whatever gifts they have to the overall task.

A culture of financial stewardship
Without embarrassment or apology we would preach on the subject of tithing on an annual basis. Jesus reinforced the principle when he challenged the Pharisees about their own practice. They tithed assiduously every kind of income, even down to the herbs in the garden, but at the same time they had neglected the more important issues of justice, mercy and faithfulness. He concluded his point by saying, 'You should have practised the latter (justice, mercy and faithfulness) without neglecting the former (tithing)'.[6] If Jesus said that the Pharisees shouldn't neglect tithing, then nor should we.

Malcolm Widdicombe, one-time vicar of Pipn'Jay in Bristol, wrote a superb little pamphlet entitled *Giving is good for you.*[7] He's very convincing in the way that he explains that ten people tithing are able to pay the salary of their minister to an average of their combined income. Another ten could support a cross cultural missionary, a further ten could maintain the church building.

It's a standard my wife and I have embraced personally in our own finances and have tithed everything from my student grant over fifty years ago to my stipend, as well as legacies, rents, gifts, pensions, profits and interest. We have been a single income family as my wife chose to work full time and unsalaried alongside me, and only once have we been overdrawn in all those years and that was by mistake.

---

[6] Matthew 23:23.
[7] Malcolm Widdicombe, *Giving is good for you* (Bristol: SS Philip and Jacob Church, 1978).

The principle of the tithe is as applicable today as it ever has been. It remains a Biblical principle and always receives the Lord's recognition. Not long ago a lady told me that she had decided to tithe her income and was surprised when her pension company contacted her a few weeks after making that decision to say that they had made a mistake in calculating what they should have been paying her and would be sending her a cheque for £10,000!

According to the Biblical standard the tithe of 10% is just the beginning of our giving and not the end of it, for over and above the tithe is the 'free will offering', that is an offering which is not required but may be given as an act of simple open hearted generosity.[8] R. T. Kendall, minister and author, is persuasive when he suggests that each Christian should give their tithe to the local church where spiritual nourishment and support are received. That then allows us to give our free will offerings to causes outside of our parish or church.[9]

When I arrived in Aberystwyth it was already an established practice to tithe the income of the church on the principle that even the Levites in the Old Testament were commanded to tithe the tithe that they received from the people.[10] If the Levites could do it in a generation when people lived very largely from hand to mouth then we should do it now. The pathway to financial blessing in any church is for the leaders themselves to tithe their income, but then for the principle to be established that the leadership tithes the tithe. So much can be done with it and it stimulates interest in the Lord's work around the world. When we give money to an organisation, we immediately want to know that the money is well used, that their accounts are in order and we want to know what progress the organisation is making. On the principle that only Christians support Christian ministry we kept a keen eye on the direction that

---

[8] See Exodus 35:29.
[9] R. T. Kendall, *Tithing: A Call to Serious, Biblical Giving* (London: Hodder and Stoughton 1982), p. 80.
[10] Numbers 18:26.

our money was being channelled to ensure that it made the maximum spiritual impact.

This principle of tithing the tithe is one which works whatever the size of the congregation; that is if the minister can get their agreement, and it then means that there is often a substantial amount of money to give away. Well resourced mission work constantly had a high profile in St Michael's as a result. Over the years a group of volunteers took aid to Poland, another to Romania and yet another to Albania. We provided financial support for a school, an orphanage and the funds to build a hammer mill in Choma in Zambia. A team went from St Michael's to build a water storage tank in Uganda.

Another of our couples from St Michael's have been building a retreat centre at Sanga Sanga, Morogoro in Tanzania. As the project began, they needed funding to buy some shipping containers to get the construction under way. We purchased two for them and one was subsequently named Borth Bog which is a Nature Reserve and Site of Special Scientific Interest just five miles north of Aberystwyth.

Perhaps the most exciting of all the projects we sponsored involved the challenge to help to build a church in Nepal. A couple from St Michael's who had been working in the area of Butwal in the south west of Nepal had helped two of the local congregations to buy land with a view to eventually getting the money together to build a church. Whilst we were there on sabbatical, we met the pastors of those congregations and came back home with the proposal that St Michael's would raise the money to help build one of the churches. We would only need £5000 and that was well within our reach. On the Sunday that we took the collection it was suggested that we should use medium sized cardboard boxes to receive the money and that they would be placed on the dais in the shape of a church building. The whole idea caught people's imagination and it was one of those occasions when the giving really was cheerful. Everyone enjoyed the imagery and the fun. When the collection was finally counted the sum was close to £23,000. We were able to build two churches for that and pay the salaries of four Nepali missionaries and four other ministry trainees for three years.

That same year of 2010 we gave away £83,850 in donations to 75 different individuals and organisations. People will say, but what will you do when you need that money yourselves later on? We will reply that those who 'are kind to the poor lend to the Lord and he will reward them for what they have done.'[11]

A culture of hospitality
Experience tells us that the dynamics of a relationship change when food is involved and when homes are opened to offer hospitality. It is a special gift and is so greatly appreciated when it happens. The non-Christian world is often impressed when it sees hospitality being offered which is not expecting an invitation in return and which happens for no other purpose than to bless those who have been invited. This is the church being counter-cultural once again.

Paul presses it home as a desirable way of life when he says, 'Practice hospitality',[12] and Peter tells us that we should 'offer hospitality to one another without grumbling',[13] as if we would grumble about it! It was because this was of such high value to us that we had so many homes where we could meet for our mid-week groups. The one value of small groups fed off the other value of hospitality. They reinforced each other.

Re-reading this list and seeking to commend each one to today's church, I cannot see one of them that I would consider to be irrelevant or inapplicable. There isn't one that I would wish to re-write or to erase from the list. If anything, I would appeal still more forcefully that they all have their place in the building of a strong church. I would perhaps give greater attention to the gift of hospitality and of eating together. In fact, I would commend the

---

[11] Proverbs 19:17.
[12] Romans 12:3.
[13] 1 Peter 4:9.

practice of a monthly 'family' church meal which keeps the entire congregation together at the end of a Sunday service. This is one of the places where relationships can be built, bonding takes place and we continue the process of nurturing our shared life.

Imagine what a church would look and feel like if these values were being actively embraced and lived out. If we can imagine it then we are imagining St Michael's, Aberystwyth over a period of twenty-five years, for that is how we were living together. Not perfectly, but it was more than an aspiration to live together in a godly way. As a result, we never had any major splits. If anyone scratched the surface of the church they found underneath what they could see on the surface which was a body of united Christians who were devoted to Jesus Christ and his kingdom's cause. Heaven on earth? No, of course not. It wasn't that good. But it was very good, just the same.

Thinking moment

- Does your church have a written set of values or some form of membership commitment? Are they Biblical or cultural? Do you think that it is desirable to have a set of values or is it unreasonable to ask too much of people these days?

- If you were going to write a set of values for your church from scratch, what would you include and what would you leave out?

Growth ceilings: paper, glass or reinforced concrete

'Many are the plans in a person's heart, but it is the LORD's purpose that prevails' (Proverbs 19:21).

For many years there has been a piece of advice about church growth which says that when the building is 80% full the congregation will stop growing. The concept behind the statement is that although there may still be room in the building, people have the perception that it has reached capacity and will choose to go elsewhere.

It is difficult to find any research which substantiates this statement, only a repetition that it is so. However, I have to admit to being staggered when I asked a relative newcomer why she had stopped coming to St Michael's and she said that the church was 'too busy'! She meant that there were a lot of people there. I can understand that for people of a shy temperament they might prefer a smaller congregation, but I have to admit that her comment rather undermined everything we had been working for at that time. Our vision was to fill our building to capacity with hundreds of people and here was a person who would have preferred it to be less full!

By 2006 we had steadily grown year on year and were clearly reversing the trend of church decline. Our Easter Sunday congregation at 11 am (which had to be counted for statistical purposes) amounted to 425 adults. The young people and children were in addition and would have raised the total to over 500. This was the largest Easter congregation in a single service for over forty years.

On our regular Sundays we had reached 80% capacity and the wardens were having to patrol the church and ask people to 'budge up' so that we could accommodate late comers. Our regular weekly attendance of different people was around 500 between the morning and the evening. A conversation had been on-going for a couple of years as to how we were to deal with the 'problem' of growth from the point of view of providing sufficient physical space.

There were a number of options to explore. One was to remove the pews and make a more flexible space on the floor of the church whilst simultaneously going upwards and providing a balcony. We looked seriously at this as an option but removing the pews meant reducing the seating capacity of the building substantially (by about 25%) and putting in a seated balcony would only return us to where we already were with the existing pews. While it would have been very useful to have a flexible meeting area, and very desirable to have additional upstairs rooms which a balcony could provide, the proposal did not solve our problems and so we looked at other solutions.

Another option was to find a larger building. As it happened a local Welsh language Presbyterian Chapel had become redundant. It was a large building seating 1000 people and that would have certainly met our needs, giving us plenty of scope for the expansion of the congregation. Not only was there more than sufficient seating in the chapel itself, but there was a vestry underneath with large meeting rooms which would have been ideal for our children's and youth ministries.

We took our church committee to look at the building and spent time inside praying and worshipping to get a 'feel' for the premises. At a subsequent meeting we agreed to make an approach to the vendors and offered £100,000 for the property. We knew that this was well below the market price, but the offer was a 'fleece' to see if the Lord was in what we were considering. It was turned down immediately as there was already considerable interest in the building as a development property. Subsequently it was sold to a building contractor but before any work could be done, it was burned down by an arsonist in July 2008.

Another option was to have two morning services with one of them including a special emphasis on families and a children's ministry whilst allowing the second one to be particularly for adults and with no facilities provided for children. This would have been a massive logistical problem for us as it would have meant doubling up on the majority of the personnel involved in delivering the services. We would have needed two worship groups, two sound teams, two vision teams, two prayer ministry teams, and two leadership teams among other things. It was very desirable and could have been possible, but it felt just out of our reach at that time.

In the event (and perhaps in the plan of God) we were overtaken by option four which was to give people away to other congregations within the parish, within the district and away from the area altogether. We used the expression 'give them away' in order to ease the pain of the substantial turn over of people that is experienced particularly in university towns. There is an annual flow of a large number of newcomers arriving in the autumn and a large number of third year students graduating and leaving in the early summer. 'Losing' people in that way created an emotional response in the heart which was not always easy to bear. We had become attached to so many over the years and then they would leave us. It was often an extremely painful experience and one that we did not enjoy.

We learned to 'give people away' through a completely different incident in Spain one summer when my wife's handbag was stolen from our car. The complications created as a result of that episode were traumatic to say the least. Cancelling the bank cards immediately, finding a translator, going to the police to report the incident for insurance purposes together with all the feelings of foolishness that we had allowed something like that to happen. The translator we had recruited was a Christian lady whom we had met in an English language church on the previous Sunday. As we were ranting on about the thieves who stole from us and the criminals who had taken advantage of us, she said quietly, 'There are a lot of poor people here in the south of Spain. Why don't you just give the money away to them?'

Her comment brought an immediate change in our mind set, and it was an approach which we applied to the people that we were continually 'losing' from St Michael's. Instead of feeling resentment that they were moving, either moving churches or moving away, we 'gave them away' and let them go with blessing and prayer. It didn't lessen the pain of the parting, but it gave us a new freedom as we blessed them on their way. Having grown as we had done to 80% capacity, having reached a growth ceiling of just over 400 in a single service, and having reversed forty years of decline we now began the process of 'giving people away.' Without us orchestrating it or planning it our congregations began to decrease in numbers. People were leaving us. So in a rather contradictory way, the more that we spoke about our growth and the 'problems' it created, the more people looked away to other churches in the hinterland of Aberystwyth as the solution!

One of the groups leaving us caused us some amusement. Our local hospital had recruited a large number of nursing staff from Kerala in southern India which is a province with a distinguished tradition of training doctors and nurses. Kerala is predominantly Christian and we benefitted from the arrival of some of them as they joined us in St Michael's. We naturally wanted to befriend them and provide them with a welcome so we invited them to the Rectory for a Sunday tea and suggested that they brought with them other colleagues from Kerala so that we could meet them as a group and hopefully integrate them into the life of the church too. In the event some thirty of them turned up in the Rectory which was a larger number than we were expecting. It turned out that many of them did not already know each other so there was a double value in the introductions that afternoon. However, the amusing outcome was that we heard subsequently that they began meeting together for worship and instead of their numbers increasing in St Michael's they actually decreased!

Perhaps if we had grasped the nettle of growth more pro-actively and more urgently then this period in 2006 would not have been one of peak attendance for us. We were not united at that time as to our vision for the future and this certainly hindered our decision making. A number of people threw out 'stingers' (those instruments with spikes on them that the police use to burst the tyres of speeding vehicles) which arrested our progress just as we felt that we were gaining momentum and a sense of direction. We should have been able to cope with those and push onwards just the same, but they coincided with the time at which the congregations began to contract. Our moment had passed.

Was there a failure of leadership and of strategy at this point? Possibly. There were two mistakes that I would not make again. One was that I always tried to avoid taking votes during committee meetings. I wanted to ensure that all of us were able to move forwards together in complete agreement with no-one left out refusing to agree with a particular decision or policy. I would try to take the 'mood of the meeting' and like the Quakers look for a consensus which would allow us to move forward with unanimous agreement. Very often our committee meetings were heavenly. I had inherited a church committee in St Michael's which was prayerful, godly and Spirit filled. They were a dream to work with and this was virtually unheard of in Wales at that time (perhaps it is still true?!). It was a testimony to the work that Bertie Lewis had done before me.

However, on reflection, I should never have adopted complete unanimity as a policy nor tried to implement it. Whilst it was loving and respectful of every opinion, in practice it doesn't really work (or didn't work well enough for us). Either decisions are delayed for too long or they are not made at all because we do not have unanimity. As we've already heard the Natural Distribution Curve tells us that there will nearly always be someone on the other side of the curve who is negative towards any proposal. Not always the same person, for that 'honour' gets passed around like the Olympic torch.

I was greatly helped when discussing this issue with a church growth advisor who said that during the war years when the

Atlantic convoys were coming from the United States they could not afford to move at the speed of the slowest because it put the rest of the convoy at risk. So what they did was to attach a Frigate to the slow ones and that provided the protection needed but it also allowed the rest of the convoy to steam ahead. If I had adopted that policy in 2006 then perhaps the outcome would have been different.

The second mistake was not to say to the ones throwing out the 'stingers', 'I respect you greatly and the points that you have made. I don't agree with you and I think that it would be beneficial if we were to meet together just the two of us and discuss this further.' That has been my policy ever since and it has always worked. Subsequently whenever there has been a difference of opinion in a church committee meeting where one or two have disagreed with a decision on an important issue, and they have been outvoted, I have made it a matter of policy to see them later privately and to talk through the issues to ensure that they know that they have been heard and that their views are respected even though the final decision may not have been to their liking.

One of the strategic decisions we did make in order to cope with substantial growth involved our Christmas Carols by Candlelight Service. This was something which had become hugely attractive in the Aberystwyth area. We augmented our regular choir with additional volunteers and included the annual nativity play into the programme. The result was a congregation of over 750. The building was absolutely packed with people standing at the back, stuffed into the side chapel and standing in the creche room in the tower. It was probably a health and safety risk because of the number of lighted candles on candelabra and window ledges. However, the atmosphere was electric and it was the talk of the town year after year.

As we had reached capacity we took the decision to have two services on the same evening with one following the other (this is probably the very decision we should have taken for our regular morning worship. Planting new congregations is recognised as one of the most effective engines of growth). So there was a nativity play included in the first service at 5 pm but still with a fully robed choir. The second service took place at 7 pm but this was an adult service only. The consequence was that the total attendance in the two services was substantially larger and it took the pressure off the building and off the content of the service allowing us a more leisurely pace to accommodate all that we wanted to do. This continues to be the Christmas pattern up until today.

Lesson learned. Make bold decisions and make them quickly. Hang about for too long and the moment may be lost. Or perhaps the Lord was in our delay? We were praying constantly at the time for heaven's guidance. The effect of 'giving away' some of our people to other churches was a blessing to all concerned. It was undoubtedly a win for the individuals and the congregations that they went to, even if it was painful for us to see them leave. We'll have to wait until we get to heaven to find out what the Lord's answer is to our uncertainties over that issue.

Thinking moment

- Is your congregation committed to growth both in numbers and in spiritual depth? What more could you do to encourage it to have that as a vision?

- Is there any one single factor which could be implemented which would make a difference to the effectiveness of your church? What could you do to help to make that happen?

Breaking the rules

'If the anger of the ruler rises against you, do not leave your place, for calmness will lay great offences to rest' (Ecclesiastes 10:4) [ESV].

I literally wept at the conclusion of a Bible reading as Kevin Roberts, Director of ReSource described the way that God breaks the rules. God breaks the rules! What a statement. What a releasing concept. Liberation! We can breathe again.

Kevin was describing how the Spirit of God had come upon the elders of the Children of Israel when they assembled for worship at the Tabernacle in the wilderness. Two of the elders named Eldad and Medad had not joined the assembly, yet they still had the anointing of the Spirit in their own tents just the same and they prophesied just like the others. News of the coming of the Spirit on these two men separately is relayed to Moses and on hearing it Joshua wants to stop them. In his view they shouldn't be prophesying if they aren't with the others. They should only do it if they are authorised. They should only do it if they are at the Tabernacle. 'Moses, my lord, stop them!'[1] says Joshua.

But Moses is a bigger man than that. 'What's up with you that you want to stop them?' says Moses, 'Are you jealous for my sake? I wish that all the Lord's people were prophets and that the Lord would put his Spirit on them!' He could have gone on to say, 'Does someone prophesying without asking me mean that I have lost leadership control and ceded it to them? Does someone prophesying in their own tent instead of in the Tabernacle undermine the specialness of this place which represents the Lord's presence amongst us? Is the work of ministry to be limited only to those who have a licence to do it?'

---

[1] Numbers 11:28.

Over the centuries the Anglican church has built up a system of rules about everything, its own Canon Law. They apply not only to what you can do, but also to what you cannot do. Some clergy say that when they were ordained they promised that they would keep the rules and that they are therefore bound by all of them. They want to keep their conscience clear on this matter, so they abide scrupulously by all of them. I can only say that whilst that sounds right and praiseworthy, I cannot join them in their approach. There's a saying that 'the fatter the rule book, the worse the organisation.' Certainly, when the rule book and its constitution take up more room on the bookshelf than the Bible we are in trouble, particularly if the rule book gets more attention than the Bible.

One of the things which repeatedly went through my mind during my time in Aberystwyth was that 'I have not been ordained to the prison ministry.' If the rules and regulations become a prison to the clergy and to the people, and stifle advance, adventure, risk, initiative and creativity then either the rules are to be broken or we're forever condemned to live in the past when those rules were formulated. The quote, 'If you always do what you've always done then you'll always get what you've always got', is attributed to Henry Ford. This principle applies as much to the Anglican Church as to the car industry.

I do not worship my conscience, I worship the Lord, and aim to be obedient to him. He is a higher authority than the rules of the church. If the rules are preventing the advance of his kingdom and holding back the presentation of the gospel then either the rules must change, or we must break them. This was one of the issues which caused Jesus so much grief. He quotes approvingly the words of Isaiah that 'these people honour me with their lips, but their hearts are far from me. They worship me in vain; their teachings are merely human rules.'[2]

---

[2] Isaiah 29:13 and Matthew 15:9.

The breaking of rules, or at least examples of extraordinary creativity towards the rules can sometimes come from surprising places. Brother Raphael was the chaplain to the University of Wales, Lampeter (as it was then called). He was also a Franciscan monk and a man with a fund of miraculous stories to tell of the Lord's intervention in his life. He was not a man who only taught the Christian faith, but he lived it too. In conversation one day he explained how the Franciscans were dealing with the issue of people who were coming to faith as adults, who had been baptised as infants but who now were looking for some kind of ceremony which included water where they could be obedient to the Bible command to believe and then be baptised.[3] His comment was that at that time the Franciscans were practising a re-enactment of baptism, so they would re-enact the new convert's baptism by full immersion where possible, using a restatement of their baptismal promises.

In a university town like Aberystwyth this was a continuous problem for us. People, especially from among the students, would come to a full personal adult faith during their time with us. Then when the issue of baptism arose some would go to the Baptists or the Pentecostals where they could be baptised without any problems because their baptism as babies was not recognised as valid. It seemed to me that the solution being offered by the Franciscans was perfect for our purposes. It was not a rebaptism which would be theologically unacceptable in an Anglican setting, but it suited the need of the young convert for some enactment of baptism which was as close as possible to what the Bible described, and the opportunity for full immersion as part of that re-enactment added to the drama of the moment. As a result, baptisms along with re-enactments of baptism were happening on a regular basis once we had installed a new baptistery tank in the church. All were expected to give a spoken testimony of what the Lord had done in their lives and the reasons why they were seeking baptism.

---

[3] Acts 2:38.

If the resolution of the problems regarding baptism came to us from the Franciscans, the resolution of the problems regarding liturgy came from Kenya. According to the rules we are only supposed to use the liturgies approved by the Church in Wales. They have been rewritten in recent years to make them more modern but using them Sunday after Sunday can sometimes lead to a monotonous and repetitive diet for any congregation.

When I first arrived in St Michael's, the evening service which was strongly youth and student orientated had been stripped down to the bare essentials. It contained a small amount of liturgy but was somewhat more flexible and varied in content. However, the morning service needed a more radical overhaul and we were greatly helped by the arrival of, what was then, a new liturgy from the province of Kenya. Dr David Gitari, one-time Archbishop of Kenya was at theological college with me in Bristol and we knew him and his wife Grace very well.[4] He was a man with an expansive mind and a serious love for the Lord. He presided over extraordinary growth in the Anglican Church in Kenya. His province had produced one of the most exciting and innovative communion services anywhere in the Anglican Communion. It's full of energy, creativity and responsiveness. It's typically African and moves with a great deal of passion and enthusiasm.

We embraced this service eagerly, particularly so because we had a substantial group of mature and godly African students worshipping with us from time to time. It provided a great alternative to the Church in Wales communion, was contemporary enough to appeal to all of the congregation, and for those who still wanted the more traditional language and forms then there was a regular communion at 8 am which would cater to their needs.

Liturgical inventiveness continued to be a feature of our church's life, and it became easier still when the overhead TV screens were installed because we didn't need to buy new books nor go through

---

[4] *Troubled but not Destroyed: The Autobiography of Archbishop David Gitari* (McLean, VA: Isaac Publishing, 2014).

the time-consuming labour of producing paper copies. It was all available to the whole congregation with a single click. A fairly continuous updating of liturgy is necessary if our weekly Sunday material is not to become over-familiar and stale.

On my very first Sunday in Aberystwyth I had a service at 10 am in the Welsh language church, in the parish, St Mair's. This was to be followed by another service in St Michael's at 11 am. Although the separate buildings are close to one another it was obvious that I was not going to be able to greet the congregation at the end of the first service or I would never be able to make the 'dash' from one building to the other. So I settled on the solution of having everything ready by 9.30 and was fully robed in vestments to meet the Welsh congregation as they arrived. One lady came into the church, saw that I was wearing the vestments and said to me, 'I'm pleased to see that you're wearing those vestments because if you didn't then I would finish with you.' Now, no minister can give in to that kind of tyranny.

I found out that the vestments had been given by a member of the congregation in memory of her father who had been a vicar, so I went to see her in the week that followed. I explained to her what had been said to me on my first Sunday and she was rightly appalled. I explained to her that from now on I would be wearing the vestments from time to time but that I would be deciding when to do so and that for several Sundays she would see me wearing ordinary robes and not the ones that she had donated to the church. There was never another word spoken by anyone on the issue. The leader has to lead. (Incidentally the lady who made those offensive remarks on my first Sunday subsequently never missed a morning service up until her death. Apparently she wouldn't finish with me after all if I didn't do what she wanted!)

That was a pretty brutal introduction to the subject of robes in the parish, but it was the first and last time that it happened. In St Michael's, Bertie Lewis had already dispensed with robes in the evening service. I was able to make the same change in the morning service too.

If Moses was presented with the problem of unlicensed prophets doing their own thing in unlicensed premises, then how were we going to handle the problem of very able preachers from other denominations who were unlicensed in the Anglican church sitting in the congregation from week to week being unable to exercise their teaching ministry? If they were to be licensed there would be a need to enquire into the nature and validity of their ordination, something which would be an insult to them. On top of this how were we going to discover the preaching talents and abilities of some of the very able people in our congregation if they were not given the opportunity to preach from time to time? The solution was to sit light to the requirements of licensing all who preach and let the call of God and the anointing of the Spirit speak for itself when these people took to the pulpit. As a consequence, we had a rich variety of preachers from very different ecclesiastical traditions.

Once a term the students would lead an evening service and one of them would preach. The sermon was always checked in advance and where necessary tidied up or even corrected. Others were also invited to preach from time to time where we could see that there was the necessary spiritual maturity and capacity to hold the attention of a congregation.

One of the ways that we introduced novice preachers to the church was to give them the opportunity to preach at the 8 am service on a Sunday morning and at the mid-week communion on a Wednesday. These were small congregations who valued a ten-minute address on one of the readings of the day. To get a student out of bed for an 8 am service was a test of their commitment as well as a test of their humility.

Within a short period of time after I had made my serious 'adult' commitment to Christ as a seventeen-year-old I became involved in the preaching teams which were sent out by Upton Vale Baptist Church in Torquay. They provided support for some of the small country chapels in the Devon countryside which were within reach of the town. This opportunity gave us experience at leading services, reading in public, taking the prayers, giving our testimonies and occasionally preaching. Those were truly formative opportunities and whilst we must have made many mistakes the local churches that we visited were always full of appreciation and commented on how refreshing it was to have young people joining them in their churches.

When in 2010 I became Area Dean of Llanbadarn Fawr, I had the chance to give some of our young and aspiring leaders in St Michael's the opportunity to do what I had done some forty years before. We organised them into teams, placed them under the pastoral care and supervision of another retired minister and sent them off to some of the vacant churches in the deanery to learn the ropes whilst still in their late teens and early twenties. We had precisely the same response to their ministry as I had had. 'How refreshing it is to see some young people with a strong faith coming to our church' was the comment we most often received. It was good for the churches that they went to and it was good for these aspiring young leaders too. All of them have subsequently ended up in the ordained ministry. When they went for their selection board interviews, they were able to go with confidence and recount the experience that they had gained.

Pragmatism wins over the rules. God breaks the rules! 'The letter kills but the Spirit gives life.'[5]

Some people might read these remarks about breaking the rules with the comment that such an attitude is indefensible and that the author should be leaving the Anglican church if he is so uneasy about the regulations of his church. My reply is that I am very happy indeed to declare my allegiance to Anglicanism. I take the same position as the late Dr Jim Packer, my one-time Theological

---

[5] 2 Corinthians 3:6.

College principal, who writes 'that Anglicanism embodies the richest, truest, wisest heritage in all Christendom.'[6] Those who know that Dr Packer had his licence withdrawn by the Bishop of the Diocese of New Westminster in Canada might call this a hypocritical statement. But the reality is that he immediately participated in the development of the Anglican Network in Canada and remained a loyal Anglican until his death in 2020.

I have been an active member of the Evangelical Fellowship of the Church in Wales[7] during all of my time in ministry in the province and have been aiming to bring an evangelical witness to church affairs both locally and nationally. In addition, I have taken immense pleasure in the formation of Anglican Essentials Wales[8] which seeks to be a pressure group of orthodox Anglicans speaking of our concerns to the church authorities. I was a member of its Council of Reference and look forward to an increasing impact from it upon the life and policies of the Church in Wales. My working principle was that it is easier to be of influence on the inside than a critic on the outside.

As the years have passed, I have appreciated Anglicanism more and more and for the whole of my ministry have commended it as a spiritual home to those who would listen and especially to those who aspired to leadership. However, I have to admit that this is becoming increasingly difficult to do in the light of the present move of the Anglican church in the west in a more heterodox direction both in teaching and in practice. Currently in Wales our leaders are committed to a progressive liberal agenda rather than to the teachings of Scripture, particularly in the area of sexual ethics.

In St Michael's we placed a high value on identifying, encouraging and training people for leadership. Several times a term I would

---

[6] 'What is Anglicanism? (J. I. Packer speaks)', https://www.patheos.com/blogs/jesuscreed/2015/03/23/what-is-anglicanism-j-i-packer-speaks/ (accessed March 2022).
[7] Founded in March 1967.
[8] Inaugural conference held in Cardiff in March 2019.

meet with those who were exploring a vocation to ordained ministry and one of our evening sessions covered twelve good reasons for being an Anglican.

A Reformed Church

We are a church which has its roots in the sixteenth century Reformation. The medieval Catholic Church was in a terrible state spiritually at the time of the Reformation and it urgently needed to be brought back to the Bible and to order its life in a way which was faithful to the teachings of Scripture. Whilst the formation of the English church under Henry VIII was chaotic to say the least, yet in its heart the roots of our church are in repentance (not Henry's) and a recognition that the church can stray. That's a healthy emphasis and one which needs to be stressed again in our own generation.

An Apostolic Church

Whatever the arguments about apostolic succession and whether or not Anglican clergy are in a direct line of succession to the original apostles, we are nonetheless an Apostolic Church. We assent to apostolic teaching and accept that the twelve apostles were uniquely placed to speak with special authority because they had kept company with Jesus, listened to his teaching, observed his life and were eye-witnesses of his resurrection. We have no hesitation in accepting that ours is part of the 'household of God, built upon the foundation of the apostles and the prophets, Jesus Christ himself being the chief cornerstone.'[9] In fact we evangelicals would appeal to the wider Anglican church today and ask it to return to a more faithful witness to apostolic teaching and not to be so selective in what it accepts of what the apostles wrote.

A Catholic Church

We are identifiably not Roman Catholics, and do not accept the authority of the pope in Rome. Yet we are at one with all Christians of every denomination in the worldwide church including Roman Catholic, Orthodox, Nonconformist or whatever, who profess a

---

[9] Ephesians 2:19ff.

Trinitarian faith. This is our privileged position as part of the 2.3 billion people who today name Jesus as Lord. That number is growing by hundreds of thousands every single day.

A Doctrinally Sound Church
Part of the foundational documents of the Anglican Church are the 39 Articles. They were produced in the heat of theological battle from four centuries ago, but they are Biblical in their conclusions. The evangelical Christian believes that the traditions of the church must be reformed by the teachings of the Bible, which was the inspiration for the Reformation in the first place. We also believe that our reason must be subject to the teachings of the Bible. It is recorded that Martin Luther made the comment to Erasmus that 'the difference between you and me, Erasmus, is that you sit above Scripture and judge it, while I sit under Scripture and let it judge me.'[10] In its formularies the Anglican church started its life sitting under Scripture and it is therefore, at its heart, an evangelical church. It is time for it to return to those Scriptures and continue to be directed and reformed by them.

A Creedal Church
Our 39 Articles emphasise the fact that the major creeds of the first four centuries of the Christian church are foundational for the belief and doctrine of every Anglican. Those creeds are repeated weekly in one form or another by the whole congregation, and they provide the parameters of faith for all of the main Christian doctrines which we hold as true. Frequently in St Michael's we would put the Apostles Creed after the first hymn and invite the congregation to participate saying to them, 'If you believe this then let's hear about it. Let's hear these words spoken loudly, firmly, confidently and with conviction.' Instead of the formal recitation of a set of propositions it became a statement of heart commitment as it was intended to be.

---

[10] David L. Edwards and John Stott *Evangelical Essentials: A Liberal-Evangelical dialogue.* (Downers Grove, IL: Inter-Varsity Press, 1988), p. 105.

An Episcopal Church
For all of our complaints about episcopal oversight, and there are many, nonetheless the ministers in our church are accountable to someone who is set over them in authority. This accountability is enormously important for doctrinal purity, as the bishops are intended to be guardians of the faith within their areas of responsibility. They should be repeatedly recalled to this task and should take extremely seriously their responsibilities before God to uphold the truths of Scripture and not undermine them. The greater the responsibility, the greater their accountability before God.[11] They are also to be pastors to their clergy providing them with support, encouragement and inspiration. The lack of accountability to some senior ministry figure who has been given oversight and authority has led to complete disaster both morally and doctrinally in some other churches and denominations. Episcopacy when it is exercised as it should be is an excellent arrangement for leadership, supervision and support.

A Liturgical Church
Whilst the 39 Articles were born out of a period of reform within the church, so too was the 1662 prayer book. Liturgically the prayer book makes explicit in prayer and in worship the doctrines which are central to our faith as Anglicans. The Articles and the 'Book of Common Prayer' are brother and sister documents. Some people find the liturgical forms rather deadening but they are there to provide inspiration for the soul and a jumping off point for our worship. They are not intended to be bars to a prison, but rather bones to provide support for the body. Whilst the flame of faith is burning low the liturgies of the church can provide a framework which is of immense benefit in sustaining the soul. Whereas when the fire of faith is burning strongly then that same liturgy can be expanded, adapted and used flexibly to enable the fire to burn still more brightly. Those churches which pride themselves on not having a liturgy usually end up with a format every bit as rigid as those who slavishly follow the same book week in week out. What's needed is liturgical freshness, freedom and flexibility to

---

[11] Hebrews 13:7.

continually renew our Sunday services and use some of the most creative and imaginative material that's available from around the world, and there is plenty to hand.

A Parochial Church
Sometimes people use the word 'parochial' as an insult. It can refer to someone who has not travelled far, who has got little experience of life and who has not seen anything of the big wide world. But the fact that the country has been divided up into parishes and ministers are put in place in those parishes to care for the people within them is an immense blessing. It means that those who live within the boundaries of that parish know who to look to for spiritual guidance and help. It means that the ministers themselves know the extent of their responsibility. They don't need to look beyond the boundaries of their parish because on the other side of the boundary, in whichever direction they look, someone else is responsible and is answerable to God for the people under their care. This can be so liberating and allow us to concentrate all of our efforts on a specific locality and a specific population. Whilst this parochial system is to some degree breaking down today as a result of the shortage of clergy, of finances and the implementation of some unimaginative strategies, nonetheless the principle has not yet been fully lost.

A National Church
We may be disestablished in Wales, but there is still a lingering memory in so many different spheres of our national life which allows the Anglican church a door of access. The opportunities to place chaplains in universities, hospitals, schools, prisons, the armed forces, local and national government and many other institutions are simply unparalleled in so many other countries. This door of opportunity is to be grasped with both hands for as long as it continues, which may not be a lot longer.

A Broad Church
Anglicanism is a bridge church between, on the one hand the historic Orthodox and Roman Catholic churches which have not

been reformed and on the other hand the Nonconformist Protestant churches. We are in a position to be able to speak to the churches in both directions and be a bridge of understanding between them. However, there are problems associated with being this middle way. The Orthodox and Roman Catholics are not convinced that the ordination of our clergy is valid and therefore our sacraments are defective. On the other hand, some evangelical groups outside of the Anglican church say that we are compromised and impure for staying within the Anglican fold. The broadness of Anglicanism has been one of its boasts in the past, but there is serious and justifiable concern now amongst many that this broadness is being pushed too far and is becoming largely meaningless.

A Christ-centred Church
The honour of Jesus is everything for us, both in the 39 Articles and also in the 'Book of Common Prayer'. There are times when this seems to get lost in all of the ecclesiastical politics and the trappings of religion, but fundamentally we are committed to Jesus as Lord. This cannot be faulted. Sometimes I have come home from a church meeting or a service and said to my wife that 'they were playing "Wendy houses" again tonight.' It was all in the dressing up and the performance and nothing more. But that isn't Anglicanism. Anglicanism at its heart is Jesus and nothing more.

An Imperfect Church
The search for a perfect church is an illusion. History has taught us that every time a group separates from the church in order to produce a congregation of like-minded people, by the time that it gets to the next generation there will be a need for further separation to preserve the purity of the original vision. Time and time again history has shown this to be true. The only grounds for separation are departure from doctrines that are central to the Christian faith or serious moral failure. Otherwise separation is

simply schism, which is a rupture in the church of God caused for no other reason than the vanity of man.[12]

Twelve good reasons to be an Anglican and to embrace Anglicanism, but still to be a maverick, something of a rebel, occasionally disobedient, colouring outside of the lines, yet nonetheless still loving Jesus and serving him. I can live with that.

Evangelical Anglicans are considered by some to be one branch of the Anglican Church. They are thought to be roughly equivalent to other branches like the Liberals or the Anglo-Catholics or the Charismatics. I believe that that is a misunderstanding of the truth. Evangelicals are not a branch in Anglicanism, they are the foundation of Anglicanism. They are the ones who are truest to the Anglican heritage. They are the inheritors of Biblical Reformed Anglicanism. A tree can afford to lose a branch or two and still thrive, but no tree can afford to lose contact with its roots. It is the evangelical Anglican who best represents our history and who has remained faithful to its theological position. Our appeal to contemporary Anglicanism in the west is not to cut itself off from its evangelical roots, otherwise it is destined to wither and die.

Let me make my point in another way with this real-life illustration. It was time to leave the forestry playground and having repeatedly told his grandson that they were going, in order to reinforce his point, the old man caught the boy by his coat and held on to him. The lad was going to have none of it and continued to pull away as hard as he could. There was a ripping sound as one of the seams gave way and the boy shouted at his grandfather, 'You're tearing my coat.' That was how the boy saw it, but he was wrong. He was the one who was tearing the coat because he was pulling away with all of his strength. The Liberals in our western church accuse those of us who are holding to traditional Biblical teaching of being the ones who are causing the coat to tear, but the reality is that having

---

[12] For further comment, see final chapter.

fully embraced the preoccupations of secular liberalism they are now practising an Anglicanism which is no longer recognisable as being true to the Scriptures. They are the ones who are 'leaving whilst staying' and they are the ones who are causing the rupture and the tearing of the coat.

The 'oath of canonical obedience' which the clergy take to their bishop concludes with the words that they will be obedient 'in all things lawful and honest.' That phrase outlines the limitations that are placed on our keeping of the rules. When the rules have the effect that people hear less of Christ, that they restrict the advance of his cause, that they lead away from the Scriptures or they focus on the institution rather than on his kingdom, then it is time for those rules to be ignored, disobeyed or even left behind.

There are considerable risks to being a rule breaker, not least being on the receiving end of the ire of one's bishop. But if things are going to change then someone has got to be a trail blazer of a new kind of Anglicanism. Dr Ralph Neighbour wrote a book entitled *'The Seven Last Words of the Church: we've never tried it that way before'* (1979). Someone has got to gather up the courage to break the mould and to pioneer a contemporary church which truly cuts the ice.

In recent years the title 'pioneer minister' has been given to some of the newly ordained clergy in the Church in Wales. That is good but not good enough. The title should not be restricted to a particular category of minister, but it should be applied to all the clergy. We urgently need pioneers who have been given permission to sit loose to the rule book and go and win our secular society back to Christ. The minister who is committed to pioneering in this way needs to take the congregation along with them so far as possible so that the breaking of new ground is a corporate enterprise with an agreed policy.

Let me give the concluding comment to that great Puritan, Richard Baxter, 'It's better that a man should be disorderly saved, than orderly damned, and that the church be disorderly preserved than orderly destroyed.'[13]

Thinking moments

- Do you think that it is ever right for a Christian to break the rules? What is the place of conscience in such circumstances because we will surely feel inwardly that disobedience is wrong, won't we?

- If there was one church rule you would like to break, which would it be?

---

[13] Quoted in Geoffrey F. Nuttall, *Howell Harris, 1714-1773: The Last Enthusiast* (Cardiff: University of Wales Press, 1965), p. 42.

Received wisdom about staff

'Don't listen to everything people say. You might hear your own servant saying bad things about you' (Ecclesiastes 7:21) [ERV].

'We haven't got a single paid employee in our church', boasted one vicar. They had a worshipping congregation of over 700 and were able to maintain all of the ministries of the church by recruiting volunteers from within their membership. That's one piece of received wisdom. Release volunteers from the congregation. Put them to work!

The other received wisdom from the church growth manuals is that for every additional hundred members in the church we need a further salaried member of staff. Perhaps an additional person to take on the pastoral work, and then another to look after the youth ministry, and then another to take on the music and worship life of the church. So growth is helped forward by increasing the size of the salaried staff. In fact, they even suggest that the staff should be put in place to initiate growth rather than as a response to it. We proved that to be correct in our own experience as the period of maximum growth in St Michael's coincided with the ministry of Andy Herrick from 2000 to 2009 (now Archdeacon of Anglesey).[1] He came on to the team as Associate Vicar and created a synergy in the leadership which was of immense benefit. This was the period of considerable advance. Every time he stepped to the microphone we knew that we could relax, whether it was in leading worship or in preaching we were in confident and experienced hands. There was not a chink of light between us theologically or experientially although politically he was Arthur Scargill to my Margaret Thatcher!

---

[1] I have broken with one of my own rules in the Preface when I said that I would not mention the name of any of my colleagues, but Andy Herrick is an exception as he was so key to our growth.

Here then are two received wisdoms standing side by side. But they say completely opposite things, one commending no salaried staff and the other commending an expansion of full-timers. Which one are we to follow? You could argue it both ways. The interesting factor linked to the first example which was not immediately apparent was that the congregation of over 700 was very largely from a middle-class professional parish. Most of the volunteers were made up of non-working wives of high earners. Their families could afford to live on just one income and there was a substantial reservoir of gifted women looking for an outlet for their energies in the life of the church. If those are the circumstances, then it is fairly obvious that no or at least very few salaried staff might be necessary.

However, if there isn't that kind of reservoir of gifted people available to be volunteers, as a church grows there is only one approach that can be adopted and that is the employing of people to hold key positions in the life of the church. Nonetheless we do need to understand that this is not the panacea for all of our problems, nor is it the guarantee of success. Having salaried staff members does not immediately bring in the kingdom of heaven. There are as many pitfalls in the employing of full-time staff as there are in motivating a team of volunteers.

Some years ago there was a Radio 4 interview between John Humphries and Sara Parkin, the former chair of the Green Party. What had happened was that in Europe their movement had gained huge publicity and a substantial following. The media were on side and it appeared as though the ball was at their feet. They were poised for political success. But then in the British general election in 1992 they had failed to capitalise on their popularity. During the course of the interview Sara Parkin was asked, 'How come that you failed after such a promising campaign?'

She replied with two very revealing comments. 'We did not plan to succeed', was the first thing that she said. What a statement. What a comment that was on our own church's experience in 2006 when our congregation peaked. We attempted planning to succeed but didn't quite pull it off. We didn't make the critical decisions quickly enough. The Green Party had done precisely the same. They had not put in place the strategy, the policies and the personnel which would have allowed them to succeed. The church must put in place personnel and finances to facilitate growth rather than wait and only respond to it if it happens.

Her second comment was equally revealing, 'We were faced with the tyranny of the volunteer.' When asked to explain what she meant she said that a volunteer is just that, a volunteer. Because they are not being paid, they come when they feel like it, and if they don't feel like it then they don't come. If something else which they consider to be more urgent comes up, then they go and do that instead. You can't complain at them because they are a volunteer. They are helping out of the goodness of their heart and not because they are being paid. You have no hold over them. You can't withhold their salary because they don't have one. Nor can you call their attention to the terms of their employment because there are no such terms. Having said this, some more progressive Christian organisations are now introducing a 'volunteer's charter' which outlines the rights as well as the responsibilities of the volunteer.

So, does having a salaried team of people make all of the difference? It certainly does when you have a dream team, and when you are leading them effectively. The problem for the majority of ministers is that they have had no training whatsoever in the art of leadership. Some people do it well instinctively. They are born leaders and hardly need any instruction, but others have to learn the hard way through trial and error, through failure, embarrassment and occasional success.

But just as we have no 'hold' over volunteers, equally we have very little 'hold' over those who are employed by our churches. Paying people a salary to work in the church is no silver bullet and does not immediately solve all of our problems. In fact, in one regard whether those who work in the church are volunteers or salaried they need exactly the same treatment. They need a vision which captivates them, which is kept fresh constantly before their eyes, and they need to know that the role that they are playing is a valuable one in making that vision a reality.

One of the principles that we embraced was to try to recruit from within our own congregation as far as possible. We should have operated that as a principle right from the outset, but it took me some time to arrive at this conclusion. The primary value of appointing from within the church was that the person stepping into ministry leadership didn't have to be taught the ethos of the church or be instructed in its history and culture which could take months if not years to fully understand. They stepped into their work, which may have been fairly new to them, but with a substantial knowledge of the life of the church, its vision and its direction. They hit the ground running. This made a considerable difference and is a principle I would try to live by now unless we failed to find the expertise that we needed locally.

In addition, we gradually produced a list of team values which applied to the staff. Every new person recruited was taken through these values by me and had them explained, the implications of them and the reason why they were there. They had all been worked out on the anvil of experience. We didn't get them from anyone else. Where there had been problems with certain members of staff in the past then the solution to that problem was included in the next list of values so that it didn't recur in the future. The longer I was in post the longer the list of values became! By the end there were twelve 'commandments' with two over-riding principles enshrined in them; firstly, the continuing spiritual growth of each staff member and secondly, the implementation of our vision for the church. Everybody who joined our staff team joined knowing what they were committing themselves to and could not argue with them at a later date.

Continuing spiritual growth.
One of the easiest bad habits to develop when we are 'professional' Christians is that because we are so engaged in the Lord's work all of the time we allow our own personal prayer life to slip. For us as a staff team we would be at worship in church on Sunday. It would be easy not to pray alone and in private that day. Then on Monday morning we would have a staff team meeting and we would be praying together again. We might think that we could miss our devotions on that day too. On Wednesday there was an early morning prayer meeting which many of the staff attended, so perhaps we could miss private devotions that day once more. Then on Thursday most of us had a day off so again we might not need to pray very extensively. That left Tuesday, Friday and Saturday for times of more extended private prayer. How easily we'd slip from walking with the Lord daily and start walking with the Lord at church meetings only.

In addition to that we were asking the 'ordinary' members of the church to add one of the prayer meetings to their weekly programme. If the salaried members of staff considered the prayer meetings to be an occasional luxury rather than a primary meeting of the week then that's the way that the rest of the church would view it. The speed of the leader, the speed of the team. So we asked that each member of staff came regularly to either the Wednesday morning prayer meeting or the one on Friday night. This was 'voluntary' and not included in their core hours, but it was an expectation that they would attend and they always did.

One of the besetting sins of Evangelicals is activism, and there is a prevailing temptation to boast about how hard we work, about the long hours that we invest in what we are doing and how little time we take off. In order to compensate for the values which we wanted to impress on our paid staff we included a paragraph in their conditions of employment which insisted that each one had a full day off from all involvement in church activities. That covered every aspect of the church's ministry including prayer meetings, worship group practices, home groups and other spiritual pursuits.

In his book entitled *Courageous Leadership*[2] Bill Hybels speaks of the three 'Cs' of team selection; character, competence and chemistry. Obviously we need someone of a godly character working with us. Obviously too we need someone who can do the job they are being employed for. But equally important is the chemistry that's necessary between the person and their minister. Is there a positive electrical charge each time that person comes walking into the room or is there an inner groan? What kind of chemistry will there be between this new person and the rest of the team, as well as the people for whom they are responsible? These are key aspects when employing new team members. It is better to have a vacancy unfilled than to have the wrong person in post.

We are aware that Christian organisations are just the same as secular ones in terms of the tensions and relationship difficulties that are experienced when people are working together in close quarters. However, there should be two prominent differences of attitude amongst Christians. The first is a preparedness to resolve offences and differences as soon as they arise and the second is to apologise and/or forgive as is appropriate so that we don't have to live with bad atmospheres. It is here that we often see the reality of personal spiritual growth when our staff members are committed to keeping their relationships in the church both sweet and godly.

Jesus himself gave us the guidance that we need in advance of trouble, 'If your brother or sister sins go and point out their fault just between the two of you.'[3] If we live by this principle then hardly anyone else will ever need to be involved in any disagreement we have. It will be dealt with between us, and that will be, or should be, the end of it. Everyone came onto our staff team with that principle in their mind and I cannot recall a single incident when I needed to remind someone that we were holding them to this principle of behaviour. Either they hid their disagreements so well from me that I never heard about them, or

---

[2] Bill Hybels, *Courageous Leadership: Field-Tested Strategy for the 360⁰ Leader* (Grand Rapids, MI: Zondervan, 2012), pp. 80-85.
[3] Matthew 18:15.

they lived by this standard. I'd like to hope that it was the latter. One way or the other friendships formed whilst on the staff of St Michael's have continued several decades later for some and will probably end up as life-long friendships too.

The implementation of our vision
Someone who was in full-time secular employment, but in addition to that was serving in the church in some capacity, would need to do their voluntary work for the church in their own time. It was something that they were giving to the church sacrificially and separately from their paid employment.

A problem for a salaried church employee is to know what they are being paid for, and what is the additional service that they are giving to the church 'out of their own time.' So, for instance, someone who is working with the finances but also helps out with the youth work on Sunday is not free to do their teaching preparation in the church office when they should be working on the finances. The preparation for the Youth Group has to be done in their own time separately from their paid work. These are some of the fuzzy edges of Christian service.

It might look as though they were then being asked to work for longer than their contracted hours; their core hours plus some more. But it was explained right from the outset that they needed to differentiate between the work for which they were employed and the ministry within the life of the church which they exercised in addition as a volunteer. We were not draconian in the implementation of this principle, but it was an important issue which needed to be identified at the beginning of someone's employment by the church.

All of us live by our diaries, and all of us live with different kinds of pressures upon us. But some use their diaries and pressures as a way of saying 'no', and that wasn't considered acceptable. It is an old adage that 'if you want something done then ask a busy person.' It may be an old saying but it's also true. It's the busy people who know how to work around their diaries and adjust their diaries to get things done. We wanted a team who were willing to make adjustments in their own schedule in order to benefit the whole work of the church. The expectation was that if the leadership asked something from the staff then their answer would be 'yes' without the sucking of teeth, the pulling out of diaries and saying 'I'm not sure if I can.' The development of a 'yes' culture was one which we constantly tried to reinforce.

One of the main dangers of employing specialists in various ministries is that we can easily de-skill and de-motivate others. Either others may think that they couldn't be as good as the paid specialists are in their particular ministry, or they may think, that the employed specialist is getting paid and I'm not, so let them get on with it. The reason for having salaried staff was not to do the work of the ministry for the congregation, but to be a focus around which the members with similar passions could gather, be involved, gain experience and release their gifts. But equally there was not to be such an excellent level of delegation that whilst the youth team led the youth event the youth minister was released to spend the evening at the cinema!

Very few teams are static for long. Most of the time there is someone who is moving on to another position somewhere else. Sometimes there is an adaptation of roles when one member of staff is discovered to have particular gifts which had not emerged earlier. Sometimes we may have to downsize the team and that is a painful experience for everyone. Not every time was the judgement sound in making each appointment despite searching interviews and earnest prayer. It is then that trial periods of three or six months become essential and shorter-term contracts are beneficial. They can easily be extended at a later date if all is going well.

In order to keep our vision sharp we had several team days spread out throughout the year, most particularly in preparation for the autumn session. We also developed a monthly Monday morning staff session when I took the lead and focussed on some particular area of our work as team. This was the opportunity to address any issues which might have arisen and encourage us to raise our game if there had been any slippage. It also gave regular opportunities to keep our vision sharp and focused.

All of our staff were given six monthly reviews when we would look at their work output in detail and check their spiritual growth. All of them were given a personal mentor who was not their line manager. The intention was that they would meet with their mentor once every two or three weeks and would have the opportunity to discuss any issues that they had in their personal lives or in their salaried work. This was of immense value. It meant that personal issues did not get mixed up with work commitments and that right from the beginning each individual knew that they were going to be properly cared for and pastored. As a result, the spiritual growth of the people who worked with us over the years was truly impressive. As a consequence, for many years we really did have a dream team.

Thinking moment

- The tyranny of the volunteer; is that how you view the people who volunteer in your congregation? How can we help volunteers to be reliable and committed? Should our churches implement some kind of written policy or charter for them?

- What would settle the manpower problems in your congregation? More volunteers or an extra paid staff member or more? What is holding back the number of volunteers? Is it lack of leadership, lack of vision, lack of resources or something else? What could be done to change that?

Evangelise or die

'The one who is truly wise wins souls' (Proverbs 11:30) [GW].

'The church which evangelises never splits' commented an experienced Bible teacher to me. As a congregation focuses outwards towards the multitudes who have not yet come to faith, they have less and less time to focus on any disagreements with one another. There simply isn't the space or energy remaining to allow people to fall out. Instead of navel gazing on their own internal problems they are vision gazing on the people outside their church who still need to hear about Christ.

But if we evangelise in order to prevent the church from splitting then that is a pretty poor motivation for getting on with the task of sharing our faith with others. Yet, in all honesty, it is better to evangelise for that reason than not to do it at all. It is surprising how low down the list of priorities evangelism can be even for the most enthusiastic of Christians.

I deliberately chose to go to Tyndale Theological College in Bristol as at the time it was the most evangelical and Biblical of the colleges in this country. I had done an academic degree in theology at university in Exeter and now I wanted to be trained for ministry in an evangelical college amongst like-minded men. Within a week or two of the beginning of my first term we were told that there was a Speakers' Corner on Clifton Downs and that there was an opportunity for open air preaching. I turned up on the first Sunday afternoon expecting to find our college well represented but there were only four of us out of our twenty-five students. A Pentecostal preacher called Felix had brought an aluminium step ladder with him and he was going full out with a congregation of skinheads around him whilst we more sedate Anglicans had a go at open-air work. No amount of encouragement, cajoling or urging increased the number of students from our college during my two years there. Even in the most evangelical of places it seemed that evangelism was low down on the list of priorities. Yet we must evangelise or die.

Unless we win the rising generation to Christ there will be no one to carry on the work of the church. Securing the future of the church would be as bad a reason for evangelising as evangelising so as not to split the church, but it is equally true. No evangelism, no future for the church.

In past generations, church growth happened to a large extent organically. The way that it worked was that children were born, baptised into the church and then brought up within it. Then they married in the church and raised their own children in the church who subsequently married and raised the next generation in the church, so the numbers increased organically. This was certainly the expectation I experienced as I began my ministry as a curate in Aberaeron in 1971; almost every young person in the town was connected to one of the denominations either church or chapel. But that system has long since broken down.

There are some who say that the church in the United Kingdom has faced this kind of problem in the past and that then there had been a spiritual change in the nation which had brought the church back into a central position in society. That is true. It is particularly true in Wales where in past generations there had been revival after revival which had a massive impact upon society. But there is absolutely no guarantee whatsoever that will continue to happen. Indeed, it hasn't happened now for more than a century. Across North Africa in the early centuries the Christian church thrived, producing some extraordinarily powerful and influential leaders; men like Augustine, Tertullian and Cyprian. It was the cradle of Christianity. But look at it today. Similarly, in Turkey. We read Paul's letters to the churches in Galatia or Ephesus or Colossae and all that remains are ruins for us to visit and a Muslim nation which has been there for centuries. The Christian faith has been largely eradicated there. We have no guarantee that something will turn up. It is evangelise or die.

It isn't just that we must evangelise for the sake of the church, but we must do it for the sake of society too. For 1500 years our national life has been structured around the Christian faith. Its morality, education, laws, and government have all been Christian. We may have strayed spiritually and morally, but it has been from Christianity that we have strayed and back to Christianity that we have often returned. Previously we knew what we had fallen away from, now we don't. There is a steady, accelerating, conscious and deliberate erosion of Christian influence at every level of our national life with progressive secular liberalism in the ascendant.

We stand back from what is happening in the nation and say, 'We must do something.' But what? The most effective thing we can do for our society is to win more people to Christ. Evangelism involves bringing the Christian message and Christian principles back into the very heart of the nation. We must evangelise in order to stop a further erosion of society and arrest its present moral decline. Our concern is not just for ourselves, but for our children and our grandchildren. Left to itself our society will not stay as it is. If we think that this is bad, then let us wait another twenty years of Christlessness and see what things are like by then.

An evangelising church has the capacity to alter society in its entirety for good. The social effects of revivals in the past are a matter of historical record. 'Save and lift' is an observable social phenomenon. A person is won to Christ, they become dependable at work, they are faithful to their spouse, they seek to raise their children well, because they are good employees they get promotion, they have a larger disposable income, they move out from the inner city, purchase their own home and their social status rises. This is a well documented phenomenon. The social implications of past revivals in Wales were substantial in many local communities where there was an increase in personal honesty, a decline in drunkenness and in all criminal offences. It was measurable, with the evidence to be found in the court records of the day. During the 1859 revival the Harland and Wolffe shipyards in Belfast had to build new sheds to hold the tools which had been stolen and were being returned. Evangelise for the benefit of our society. It's a no-brainer. Change the world one life at a time.

All too often the church is indifferent to the plight of people who are outside of it, when it is clear from the Bible that the responsibility for the blood of those who are lost, is on the shoulders of those who have already been found. This is the teaching of Ezekiel: 'If anyone hears the trumpet but does not heed the warning and the sword comes and takes their life, their blood will be on their own head. ... but if the watchman sees the sword coming and does not blow the trumpet to warn the people and the sword comes and takes someone's life, that person's life will be taken because of their sin, but I will hold the watchman accountable for their blood.'[1]

The focus of attention for Christians should be on the people who do not come to worship rather than to create a comfort zone for those who do. Jesus made it plain that even if there were 99 in and one was out then the one that was lost would receive the benefit of his entire attention.[2] The 99 would be left whilst he went looking for the one remaining sheep. But we have one in and 99 out! The statistics are the other way around. How much more must we go after the ones who are not in, in order to become truly Christ like.

When we get to heaven there are two men I shall be looking out for. One is the Reverend David Abernethie who was the preacher that Sunday morning when the direction of my life was changed. The other is Jim Stokes who led my Crusader Bible Class. He prayed for me and the other boys and modelled Jesus to me as a youngster. I owe an enormous amount to them. I wonder who will thank us for what we contributed to their coming to faith and growth in faith?

In his book *The Hour that Changes the World* Dick Eastman writes, 'Our supreme purpose is to glorify God and our supreme task is to

[1] Ezekiel 33:4-6.
[2] Matthew 18:12-14.

evangelise the lost.'[3] It is clear from the Bible that not everyone has the same destiny after death. Jesus spoke about two alternative destinations for people. He spoke about weeds and wheat,[4] and about sheep and goats.[5] Jesus also made it clear that we are the deciders of our own destiny. Our destiny is based on our response to him, and what we choose to do about his teachings. No-one is forced to go to heaven. The universalist who says that everyone will eventually end up there is suggesting that God will over-ride our free will and save even people who don't want to be saved.

Others suggest that there will be a second chance after death. They say that we will all see the spiritual realities which at the moment are only dimly seen and we'll all be more ready and willing to believe. Certainly, there will be no more agnostics or atheists within the first minute of the next life. But if there is a second chance why does the Bible give such a sense of urgency to the Christian message? Why should men like Paul have risked their lives and ultimately sacrificed their lives? Why weren't they much more laid back about it all? Why does the Bible say that now is the day of salvation,[6] and now is the time for decision? Here's the reason. It is written in the epistle to the Hebrews: 'People are destined to die once, and after that to face judgement.'[7] Evangelise or die.

Yet we still haven't reached the most important reason for evangelising. It surely is simply because we love people. If we are to love our neighbours as ourselves then this is the supreme way of demonstrating our love. My neighbour doesn't know why he's here, where she's going, doesn't know what life is about, what his destiny is going to be. She is in confusion of mind and is spiritually lost. When Luis Palau, the Argentinian evangelist, came to Wales

---

[3] Dick Eastman, *The Hour that Changes the World: A Practical Plan for Personal Prayer* (Grand Rapids, MI: Baker, 1978), p. 75.
[4] Matthew 13:30.
[5] Matthew 25:31-46.
[6] 2 Corinthians 6:2.
[7] Hebrews 9:27.

for a mission some years ago he was interviewed on the radio rather aggressively and asked the question, 'Don't you think that it is arrogant for you to come to Wales and tell people that they are lost?' Palau replied, 'I'm not. They are telling me that they are lost.'

The love of Christ constrains us to evangelise. Our love for him. We want to obey him and do what he has asked of us. But also his love is in us, so we want to tell others because we care about them and their eternal destiny. We are constrained to speak out of love. Bishop J. C. Ryle summed it up in this sentence, 'The highest form of selfishness is that of the man who is content to go to heaven alone.'[8]

A hundred years ago bringing in the harvest was not the work of one farmer but rather a community enterprise. The day before the harvest was cut, messages would be sent around to the neighbouring farms. Early in the morning on the following day the men would gather. They would have brought their own scythes. They would stand together spending the first minutes of the day sharpening their tools and sharing the most recent gossip. Then they laid their jackets down with their backs to the hedge and slowly side by side they began to swing their scythes with a rhythm which would continue throughout the day. Within an hour or so their wives would arrive and they would follow the men across the field collecting the corn, binding them into sheaves and then stacking them into stooks.

These men would need food constantly throughout the day. So by breakfast time the grandparents and the children would come from the farmhouse bringing with them the first meal of the day. Everyone would sit down to eat. Community was built. Then the same thing would happen in the middle of the morning and at mid-day, and then again in the afternoon for tea, and then a further meal in the farmhouse to conclude the day's work after dark. Everyone

[8] J. C. Ryle, *Bible Commentary: the Gospel of Luke* (Editora Dracaena, 2015) p. 145.

was involved from the youngest to the oldest, the men and the women. On harvest day it was a whole community enterprise. Later the favour would be paid back to the neighbours on the day that their harvests were gathered in.

Evangelism is a whole church enterprise. Paul may have advised his convert Timothy to 'do the work of an evangelist',[9] but he would have been horrified at the thought that the work of evangelism is restricted to a particular individual or a particular group of people within the church and that others devote their time, energy and efforts to other things.

There are two special responsibilities which every single Christian is able to fulfil. One is to respond to Peter's very simple instruction, 'Always be prepared to give to everyone who asks you the reason for the hope that you have.'[10] The other responsibility is to be an inviter. Guest services were part of the regular pattern of our church life from the outset in Aberystwyth. It's comparatively easy to structure a service around a particular theme and then to advertise it widely through fliers, posters, social media and personal invitations. These guest services took on a new form once we had adopted the philosophy of Seeker Services from the Willow Creek Community Church in Chicago. The services were stripped of parts of the liturgy which would have caused difficulties to an uncommitted guest. So the confession prayer which contains expressions of repentance was removed on these occasions. So too, the recitation of the Apostles Creed.

Similarly, any extended prayer time during the service had to be reduced considerably. Much of what took place was presentational in style. Interviews, readings, dramatic sketches, musical items and illustrated addresses were the order of the day. Many of the hymns and songs were chosen because they would have been familiar to the majority of people. Some of them still linger in the public consciousness in the local pubs and at rugby matches. Our

[9] 2 Timothy 4:5.
[10] 1 Peter 3:15.

music group would play and sing some contemporary Christian songs which had particular relevance for the theme. Occasionally we would play a secular song from which a specific spiritual point was going to be made.

Because we had a particular focus for these services they flowed with a sense of purpose and direction to them. We covered subjects like 'All alone in an empty universe?', 'Christians make the best lovers', 'The occult: alright or all wrong?', 'Is God a delusion?', 'The Da Vinci Code: Dan Brown or Damn Brown?', 'Who can we trust: bankers, priests, journalists?'

We were one of the early parishes in Wales to adopt the use of the Alpha course as our primary evangelistic tool with over 90 coming on our first course. We used the programme flexibly and adapted it to our own local circumstances but as a strategy it constantly 'produced the goods.' One of the hardest things for me was to give the Alpha Course away to other leaders in the church. I was very reluctant because I found myself so motivated and inspired by it, but it became necessary as the demands of leadership in the parish grew.

In-reach was one means of evangelism with our Guest Services and Alpha Courses, but out-reach was going to be served in other ways. We were continually looking for inventive ways to touch the local community with the Christian message. For several years we wrote, published and delivered a church newspaper called *The Angel*. Historically the parish of Aberystwyth had a magazine, however, it fell on hard times as the cost of printing continued to increase making it difficult to sustain, and anyway it was a publication for church members only, paid for by subscription. A suggestion was made that we should replace it with a newspaper which would be free with the cost of production coming from advertising revenue. It was intended to be tabloid in form with plenty of pictures, reduced text and visually attractive as well as easy to read and would be published three or four times a year.

As an exercise in getting information out into the local community it was excellent and fulfilled all that we wanted to do. The front page was often devoted to the testimony story of one of our church members who was well known in the local community. We would also cover national or even international issues from a Christian standpoint. There was information about the life of the church including information on things like our marriage courses, youth clubs and other activities. It was delivered free to every home in the parish and was a very valuable tool.

Whilst we continued to do small scale evangelism including door to door visitation and open-air services on the promenade and in the town centre, we also initiated large scale missions. Canon Michael Green returned to Aberystwyth and brought a team of students with him from Wycliffe Hall Theological College in Oxford.[11] They came to join us for 'Holy Week' and participated in an interdenominational programme of events.

In discussing with him what our usual approach was to 'Holy Week', involving a service every evening from Monday to Thursday and then a full series of services on Good Friday he was very dismissive. That wasn't nearly adventurous enough for him. With a wave of the hand he rejected the proposal of a 'standard' Holy Week, so it was deconstructed. In the event we had ninety different meetings and activities across all of the churches of the town, we touched the lives of over 4000 people during the week, there were more than 350 people filling the main street of the town for our march of witness on Good Friday and we had a congregation of 850 in the Great Hall of the university for our final service on Easter Sunday evening. It was classic Michael Green. Energy, enterprise and creativity bursting out in every direction.

We were able to use that as a model during March 2007 when our Diocesan Bishop brought the ordinands from the St Davids diocese for a mission with a similar style.[12] This too involved a large

---

[11] Holy Week 1999.
[12] 'In from the cold' mission during 'Holy Week', 18-27 March 2007.

number of home meetings of various kinds as well as a reception with the Mayor and Town Council, activities for youth and children, and a concluding service in the Great Hall of the university. Part of the reasoning in my mind for this mission was to give the future ordained leaders of our diocese a taste of what it looks like to be active in an evangelistic enterprise. Whilst we had a broad cross section of theological outlooks represented amongst the team it was nonetheless an important initiative for them to be involved in.

One of the last missions in Aberystwyth before my retirement was on a substantially larger scale, for we were not just looking to evangelise locally, but right across the whole of south-west Wales. It was suggested that we invite Daniel Cozens, one of the Archbishop of Canterbury's Six Preachers, who was at that time the initiator and leader of the Walk style missions which had already taken place all over the country. This one which we would host in the counties of Carmarthenshire, Pembrokeshire and Ceredigion was to be called 'Walk St David'. It would begin in the cathedral and then move slowly north with a week in each county during October 2010. Aberystwyth would have a team coming to lead a whole variety of meetings and enterprises around the town and district. Amongst the many activities was a door-to-door visitation with a personal belief's survey. Information gleaned from the responses on the doorstep was later collated and published in our *Angel* newspaper.

As a consequence of the size of the congregation in St Michael's and the commitment of so many people it was comparatively easy to draw together teams to go to other parishes across Wales. The St Teilo's Trust was formed in 1994 and existed for the encouragement of evangelism exclusively in Wales. I was invited to be a non-salaried evangelist, and requests for help with missions and evangelistic activities came in from right across the whole of Wales over a period of more than twenty years.

Our commitment from Aberystwyth was to be a resource church for mid-Wales as well as a blessing to the nation overall, so for a number of years at the beginning of the summer vacation our two student pastors would take a team of students to be involved in evangelism in a parish context somewhere else in Wales. The result was energised Christians returning with stories to tell. That is a mirror image of the disciples of Jesus returning to tell him what had happened to them when he had commissioned them to go and minister in the villages of Galilee.[13] This is the Master's pattern.

On one occasion my wife and I were on holiday in Pitlochry in Scotland and visited the Edradour whisky distillery. They had a heritage centre at the distillery and we were taken on a guided tour and given a brief history of single malt whisky. That's the first time that I have ever seen a man with a truly red end to his nose. Our guide had clearly had too many drams at the end of each of the tours that he had been conducting. As we were going around the centre, I could not hold myself back from thinking that we had a far better story to tell than that of single malt whisky but that no-one in Wales was telling it.

On our return home we began to explore the possibility of establishing a Welsh Christian Heritage Centre which we would erect every summer season in the back of St Michael's Church. With the help of staff from the National Library of Wales we produced thirty panels telling the story of the arrival of the Christian faith in Wales with the Roman legionaries, right up until the present day. It first opened in July 1996 and there were panels telling of the influence of the saints in the early days of Christianity here, panels telling the story of the monasteries, the coming of Protestantism, the history of the revivals, the influence of the industrial revolution and the transformation brought about by secularism in recent years.

'The Cross and the Dragon' was the title of a half hour film that we had commissioned telling the same story but using the visual

---

[13] Luke 10:17.

techniques of a professionally made film. This was shown on a permanent loop during the summer on a large screen television in the church which was open throughout the day and staffed by volunteers. Our visitor numbers increased in the church as a result, and the information panels were put on loan to various institutions both in north and south Wales.

Perhaps the greatest bit of fun was our 'Evangelistic Ice Cream' initiative. We hired an ice cream van which was sited permanently during the summer months at the far end of our church car park close to the children's swings alongside the castle. The idea was to sell ice creams, lollipops and cold drinks, and to give an invitation to our church services or to invite people to visit the building whilst they were close by. We also gave invitations for children to our Beach Mission which was taking place in the Band Stand on the promenade. As an enterprise it always broke even financially and was such fun to do.

So what was the result of all of this evangelistic activity? Did people become Christians? Yes, they did. Not hordes at every event, but there was nothing that was unproductive. Doors were opened for people to hear about the church, hear about the Lord and come in. And they did.

However, perhaps the most influential evangelistic event that was held was our weekly Sunday services. I'm almost surprised when I write that sentence. We really do underestimate the value of what we do week by week. As I reflect on all of this evangelistic activity, there isn't a single mission or enterprise that we were engaged in that I would not do again, but the place where I would put more prayer and more effort and more intentional evangelism would be the Sunday services. It was there as people came in and were welcomed with genuine care, and witnessed engaging and sincere worship, and listened to the Bible being explained; it was there that the miracle of conversion seemed to happen most often. Good for Sunday church, I say. Let's have more of it.

It was Canon David Watson who brought the attention of the church back to the evangelistic power of a congregation engaged in soul-stirring worship. When an 'unbeliever' observes Christian people completely absorbed by their Lord and offering to him exuberant worship then at the very least questions are raised in their minds. What is going on here? What is happening? Is this real? Are these Christians making genuine contact with God? Those who come back repeatedly will be drawn to know and to love the one who is being worshipped.

It was because of the evangelistic power of worship that whilst we stripped away many of the other parts of the liturgy which invited a congregational response when we were having our guest events (seeker services) we did not entirely follow the Willow Creek pattern and take out the worship part of our service. There was too much value in retaining it as a central feature of what we were doing.

I found it fascinating to visit the Willow Creek Community Church in Chicago in the Spring of 1995 and also to spend some time in the Airport Vineyard Church in Toronto where the 'Toronto blessing' was taking place. It seemed to me that both churches were being massively effective but that they were using two different strategies. In Chicago they were going to the heart through the mind. Everything was very cerebral. The appeal was to the thinking person. They wanted to make a case for the Christian faith and to explain the relevance and practical application of the Christian faith. However, in Toronto they were going straight to the heart, and through the heart to the mind. Their emphasis was upon experiencing God, and the mind came in afterwards trying to come to terms with what God had already been doing in the heart. From the mind to the heart on the one hand, and from the heart to the mind on the other.

But what if we could build a church where both were happening simultaneously? Where the Christian faith was explained clearly and rationally, but where also those who attended were given the opportunity to experience the Lord through worship and personal prayer ministry. That was what we aimed to do week by week. And we saw the results.

The church must evangelise or die. It is as stark as that. The church which has seen no conversions over a period of twelve months has died a little bit because all of the members have become twelve months older. It is artificial to increase our congregation by transfer growth. New people moving into the area and coming from other churches are always welcome, but that it not real growth. The kingdom of God only grows when people are being converted and becoming disciples of Jesus. If we do not evangelise this current generation and win them for Christ the church will be finished in Wales and across the country by the next generation. Evangelise or die.

Thinking moment

- Where does evangelism fit in your church's list of priorities? Where do you think that it ought to fit?

- Evangelise or die: is that a realistic assessment of where we stand or is it unnecessarily negative? How do you think the current decline in church attendance can be addressed and reversed?

Stopping the revolving door syndrome

'Hope deferred makes the heart sick, but a longing fulfilled is a tree of life' (Proverbs 13:12).

Every church has some experience of the revolving door syndrome. Someone new turns up at a service. Then they come back a second time. Then we see them on a more frequent basis and begin to think of them as regulars. They might even join an Alpha course or a home group but then just as suddenly as they came they disappear again. No amount of pastoral contact brings them back. It was just as though they were doing an evening class at the Further Education college. They completed their ten weeks on goat keeping for beginners, or brush up your Spanish, and then they moved on to something else. The revolving door has completed its circuit, they came in through it, stayed inside briefly, but then the door turned 360 degrees and tipped them out onto the street once again.

Put that very common experience alongside the statement of Jesus when he was speaking in prayer to his Father and said, 'I have not lost one of those you gave me.' He says the same thing twice according to John's Gospel.[1] That's all very well for him but what about us? That's not our experience. We have lost many who it seemed the Lord had given us. I read those words of Jesus with a heavy heart and cannot echo them after five decades of ministry.

Stopping this revolving door from happening is a major issue for many churches. We never completely resolved the problem in St Michael's because we were dealing with human beings, but we did get better at it. One of the questions I wrestled with for several years was to work out where my responsibility lay in pastoring the people who came to worship and keeping them within the church. How is the responsibility apportioned? If it is 100% God's responsibility, then I don't have to do anything at all. If they come,

---

[1] John 17.12 and 18.9.

they come and if they don't, they don't. If God has chosen them then they'll stick and if he hasn't then they won't. But that doesn't feel quite right. That smacks of fatalism rather than either election or predestination.

So, where does the responsibility lie? Is it 50% God's responsibility and 25% my responsibility as the minister, and 25% their responsibility as the person in question? That makes me feel a bit better but I'm not sure that view isn't a cop out. It feels as though I'm trying to shrug off some of the responsibility. Or is the responsibility divided equally between us all? 33.3% to God, 33.3% to me and 33.3% to the person involved? But that doesn't seem right either. Surely God has got a bigger part to play in all of this than I have.

The solution it seems to me lies in the fact that it is 100% God's responsibility, and 100% my responsibility and 100% the individual's responsibility. The Lord offers his maximum commitment to the individual, so too does the minister, but then the individuals themselves have to offer 100% of their commitment back to the Lord. Anything less than that means that we are looking at a disciple who will not flourish.

As part of my 100% responsibility, I need to do a number of things. (Perhaps I shouldn't, but I am taking it for granted that this is a matter of prayer for the minister and the congregation). One thing that is essential is for me to provide an environment in which relationships can be formed and deepened. I cannot make friends for someone else. How many times I must have said that over the years. But I can provide a place where friendships can be formed.

Within the small group life of the church, in just a few weeks friendships can begin to blossom which is why we placed such a high value on them. In looking at the Bible together, in discussion, worship and prayer a bond begins to form and trust begins to develop. There is an accountability, an expectation of one another, an intimacy as each one discloses more of themselves to the others.

Here is the basic unit of pastoral care within the church, but it is also the basic unit of community.

The work of a bricklayer is quite skilled but the actual theory of bricklaying is simple. Two bricks have been laid side by side in the new wall, over the join between the two a new brick is laid, then there is a brick laid at either end of the new brick, but then for that brick to be held in place it needs to have two bricks up above with the join in the middle once again. That way each brick in the wall has contact with six other bricks, two below, one at either end and two above, and it is held in place by all six. If any one of those bricks is missing the wall will still stand but it will be weakened. If every Christian is close to six others in the church then the possibility of them staying over the long term is increased massively. Touched by six others and touching six others. That sounds like a recipe for permanence and continuity.

Fellowship
The value of fellowship has been seriously underestimated by us. All too often we think of fellowship as having a cup of coffee and a chat together after the Sunday service. Fellowship is substantially more than that. Fellowship is close to being something sacramental, a means of grace, one of the ways that God gets through to us. At its heart is the opening of the Bible and the shared learning from its pages, but fellowship goes much deeper than even that. It is the listening to the experience of another Christian for whom something special has happened in the previous week and being inspired by that story. It is the arrival of some spiritual truth in the mind and heart of another person with that realisation, the 'Oh, I see it.' Then reflecting on what we hear we begin to think to ourselves, 'That could be me.' Or 'if God can do that for her then he could do something similar for me.' Or 'God is real after all and still at work in the world.' We go away from a conversation like that filled with expectation, with our faith level raised, and with the hope that the next time we meet it may be me that brings a new story of the way that God has been involved in my life or some new insight and realisation. That is fellowship.

An inspiring meeting of Christian lives leading to a deepening in faith, a hunger for more and a raised expectation. This is what the small group life of the church should be all about and the results which flow from fellowship.

The Methodists long ago had their 'experience meetings' where the members shared with one another what the Lord had been doing in their lives. Their emphasis on a 'felt Christ' was one on which everyone agreed. This is at the heart of our Christian experience and means that we have so much to offer to others of what we ourselves have encountered in our personal lives.

Testimony

Another one of my responsibilities as the minister is to provide a context in which each person has the opportunity to speak publicly of their faith, how they have come to faith and the reasons for their commitment to Christ. This too is extremely important. Paul in his letter to the Romans says that we need to confess with our mouth that Jesus is Lord, as well as believe it in our hearts.[2] The public verbal nailing of our colours to the mast is hugely beneficial to the individual and also to the wider church. The individual is strengthened and increases in confidence by doing it. The faith of the congregation soars when they hear the faith story of another person, particularly if it is recent. God is at work in their midst.

We need to get new Christians on their feet to testify to the rest of the membership at an early stage in their commitment to Christ. There is something again which is almost sacramental in this public declaration of faith, and it is honoured by the Lord when it happens; everyone benefits.

Baptising early

One of the other areas where I believe we were weak in our responsibility to new Christians was in failing to offer to baptise them quite quickly or to re-enact their baptism if they were christened as a child. On the Day of Pentecost Peter did not just

---

[2] Romans 10:9-10.

invite his congregation to repent, he also invited them to be baptised that day as an outward and visible sign of that repentance.[3] Three thousand of his hearers responded to that invitation, probably using the large numbers of *mikvas* ('ritual baths') to be found to the south of the temple in Jerusalem. Repentance and baptism go hand in hand.

I am aware that there is a counter argument that the reality and seriousness of a person's repentance needs to be tested over a period of time to ensure that it isn't just an emotional spur-of-the-moment response. There are good reasons for the catechumenate and for having an opportunity to teach someone the faith over a sustained period of time. But we cannot escape the New Testament experience of preaching for a response, and when the response is made then it is sealed in baptism immediately. Philip baptised the Ethiopian on the day that he believed.[4] Ananias did the same with Saul[5] and Peter the same with Cornelius.[6] There was no lengthy course of instruction, and for each of them this was their public declaration that Jesus was Lord of their lives.

I know that some Pentecostal churches practice immediate baptism upon confession of faith, and there is much to commend it. I admire them for their courage in this kind of obedience, not least because we have clear and repeated Biblical precedent for it. We never practised this in St Michael's because of the physical complications of having robes available and the water in the baptistery heated but I still view it as the ideal.

Providing opportunities to serve
Another responsibility on the part of the minister towards the new Christian is to find an area of service within the life of the church which is commensurate with their giftings. We know that every Christian has three different levels of gifts. There are the ones that

[3] Acts 2:38.
[4] Acts 8:38.
[5] Acts 9:18.
[6] Acts 10:48.

we are born with. We speak of people being naturally gifted. With these gifts being consecrated to the Lord for use in his church everybody wins. It ties the new person into the life of the church, gives them responsibility and makes them feel wanted. Tragically in some congregations the only way for some people to get their gifts released is to wait for thirty years and then they'll be accepted. Such an attitude has to be consciously challenged and deliberately broken by the minister. That approach cannot be allowed to continue otherwise there will be gifts lying unused, congregations robbed of the whole ministry of the church, members feeling that they have no role to play in the life of the church, and others unnecessarily burdened as they try to carry responsibilities and tasks which should be shared more widely in the congregation.

Not only are there natural gifts, but there are our acquired gifts, abilities that we have learned through our family background or have been taught in school or college, or through an apprenticeship. We may not sparkle in these particular areas as we do in the gifts with which we have been born but nonetheless we are competent and able to function well. These too are gifts to be harnessed and released for the blessing of the church.

Then thirdly there are the gifts of the Holy Spirit which are supernatural. As the Spirit came, so he came bearing gifts for the individual to use for the building up of the church. They are not gifts for the individual to possess and hold to themselves, but gifts which are for the blessing of the entire congregation. The rediscovery of these spiritual gifts in the life of the church in the last fifty years or so has led to the explosive growth of the church around the world. 'Do not put out the Spirit's fire'[7] writes Paul and when the minister welcomes and enables the release of these gifts so the church prospers.

Had Paul been converted in some of our churches today rather than on the road to Damascus long ago then he would have been put into cold storage for a number of years in order to prove that he really

---

[7] 1 Thessalonians 5:19.

was a serious and committed disciple. Instead what happened was that having been healed of his blindness and baptised he 'began at once to preach in the synagogues that Jesus is Lord'.[8] He baffled the Jews in Damascus with his preaching not just because of the persuasiveness of what he had to say but because they knew that literally days before he had been of a different mind. His conversion was as difficult to believe as the convictions he was now sharing with them.

This principle of discovering people's gifts and releasing them in the church does not mean that we suddenly place new Christians into positions of leadership and authority within the local church. Paul was clear that the work of an overseer is not to be given to a recent convert who might be in danger of becoming conceited.[9] He also cautions against laying hands suddenly on someone, presumably for the commissioning for a particular ministry.[10] However, these words of caution do not undermine the point which is that we need to trust the integrity of someone's commitment to Christ and encourage them to release all of their gifts in his service as soon as is practicable.

Prayer ministry
If we are going to offer holistic ministry to our congregations then we need to give evidence of our concern for the whole person. We are people who believe that prayer is effective, that God listens to us and that he responds to our prayers. So the ministry of praying for people, praying with them about their needs, calling on the Lord to answer them and send his Spirit to heal, restore, intervene, empower; this will surely be effective. We can expect to see results and outcomes. This too will assist in closing the revolving door because the church becomes a place where people can come for help, be treated seriously and with compassion, be prayed with and for, and see the results which come from such prayers. Remarkable

---

[8] Acts 9:20.
[9] 1 Timothy 3:6.
[10] 1 Timothy 5:22.

things happened in St Michael's as a consequence of the prayer ministry team which was formed in 1996.

Prayer ministry was already being offered on an informal basis when I first arrived in Aberystwyth. The church leaders would pray with those who identified themselves as being in need at the close of the service. Others too amongst the more mature members of the congregation would instinctively be offering to pray for those who expressed a need. 'Shall we pray together about that problem?' was an invitation being frequently offered as a gesture of love and compassion.

There are clearly many concerns when prayer ministry is offered in an informal setting, not least that this can easily become the happy hunting ground for the wild and the wacky. Slowly and deliberately we began to provide a more formal setting in which prayer ministry could be offered by trusted members of the congregation. Initially, responsibility for a particular Sunday was passed around on a rota basis to reliable home group leaders who would take their turn in this ministry. They would recruit members of their group in whom they had confidence and they were released for this work week by week.

After a time it became increasingly clear that we needed to recruit a specialist team, partly for the sake of proper training, partly for the need for an identifiable group to conduct the ministry, partly to ensure that we were covering all the safeguarding concerns which have become increasingly important, and partly for the sake of continuity. The formation of the prayer ministry team under one of our senior leaders was one of the most important features of the spiritual progress of the church. It meant people were genuinely cared for, their needs were taken seriously, there was long term support for them and that the miraculous could still happen and did! This aspect of church life continues to be important twenty-five years later.

Family life
One of the emphases that we worked hard to constantly reinforce in St Michael's was our sense of the congregation being like a family. Again this is a clearly Biblical concept with both the apostles Paul and Peter speaking of the family of God, and the household of faith.[11] We spoke often about the 'family of St Mike's.' We did not create the family because it already existed. The family is created the moment that we begin to address God as 'Our Father'. Those two words make us into children of the one Father, part of the same family. We were his family of St Michael's because that is the building in Aberystwyth in which we met. We preached it and we attempted to practice it week by week.

This was a value we wanted to continually emphasise. So we did things that families do. We ate together often. We took any opportunity for a celebratory meal whether it was pancakes on Shrove Tuesday or a special meal on Mothering Sunday or a Harvest Supper or just coffee and pudding. Food was central. It was a bonding experience.

'You can choose your friends but not your family,'[12] wrote American novelist Harper Lee. We know what she was saying. We don't get to decide who we have in our families. We know what families are like too. Everyone has a mad auntie, cousins that don't get on, a disreputable sibling, in-laws who are awkward. That's the nature of a family. But our Christian family was going to be different. Different because of the effort that we would make to be of one heart. Different because we would choose to love each other. Different because everyone would count. Different because there would be a place for everyone. The singles would be as important as those who were married and the childless as important as the families with multiple children. The elderly would be respected and loved and provided for just like the youth and the children. Those with mental health problems would be considered

---

[11] Titus 1:7, 1 Peter 4:17, 1 Thessalonians 4:10, 1 Peter 2:17.
[12] Harper Lee, *To Kill a Mockingbird* (1960) (New York: HarperCollins, 2002), p. 256.

as important as the high-flying academics and wealthy businessmen. Everyone in this family will be equally valued.

We began to feel that we were making real progress in identifying ourselves as a church family when the students began to refer to my wife as Auntie Pru. Not only was this a term of endearment but it established in their minds their own participation in the family.

Families keep in touch with each other, so even when people left Aberystwyth and moved away there would still be that network of friendships which had been established, those six bricks in the wall would still be in contact and news would filter back into the life of the church. As a consequence, we had a 'church family in the dispersion', not just across the British Isles but across the world touching all six inhabited continents. Some of them had become Christians amongst us, others had learned to pray in our prayer meetings, others had released their gifts in service amongst us, others had been filled with the Spirit.

We had established a prayer commitment to those who had left us, and when the sixth edition of a prayer bulletin entitled 'Ministries we support' was produced for St Michael's in 2012, it contained 117 names of people who had either been ordained or who had gone to work overseas in some capacity or another, and we knew that that was a conservative figure.

In addition to the prayers for those we had sent out we began a programme of pastoral visitation of our diaspora. Whilst on sabbatical in 1994, my wife and I visited one of our former students in Xian in China. During a meal together she remarked that, 'I would rather have you here with me than £3000 put into my bank account'. That statement sparked a commitment from us to attempt to visit all of our St Mikes family who were working overseas for the Lord. That was the moment of realisation that this ministry of pastoral visitation was hugely important. It was reinforced by a comment from a Christian worker in Thailand who confided with tears in one of 'our' missionaries that no one from her home church had been to visit her in fourteen years. If we had known before how valuable and important this was, we would have started sooner. A late developer again! Since then we have been to New Zealand, Spain, France, Germany, one of the Central Asian Republics, Uganda, Tanzania, Zambia, Kenya, Thailand and India to visit 'our' people, the family of St Mikes in the dispersion.

So did we get it right? Of course not. But we did get it right some of the time. What I can say is that we had a fully Biblical church just like the one which Jesus described for us in close detail in his parable about the sower.[13] In that parable Jesus was not teaching theology or a Sunday School lesson, he was teaching church life, congregational life. This is the way that the local church is going to be, he was saying. Listen to my parable, look at your congregation and you will see that the two things correspond closely to each other. That's the church we had, a church with heart-breaking tragedies and a church with glorious successes. All of the categories that Jesus described were represented amongst us from those on the fringe who never made it, from the shallow responders who came in and went out again, from the ones who had their faith strangled out of them, to the fully committed and fruitful. A church which Jesus foresaw in detail in his parable. Real church. In amongst it all were some of the most lovely and godly Christians you could ever meet anywhere in the world. They didn't make a show of their Christian faith. They won't have their names on any list of saints on this earth, but they were truly saintly and it was an honour to know them, to minister to them and to be a part of their spiritual family.

And the best part of this story? It isn't finished yet, for the end of this story has not been written. It continues even today with some of the hard ones softening, some of those who went out through the revolving door coming back in again for the second time, some of those who had their faith strangled are untangling themselves from the world and coming back, some of those who were bearing fruit thirty-fold are now bearing fruit sixty-fold, and some of those who

---

[13] Matthew 13:1-23.

were bearing fruit sixty-fold are now bearing fruit a hundred-fold, and some of those who were bearing fruit a hundred-fold have gone home to glory! We know their names and so does the Lord.

Thinking moment

- Is your congregation familiar with this problem of the revolving door? What is the primary reason for it? What could be done to stop it from happening in your church?

- What can be done in your church to create a greater sense of family? Can you name six people who are holding you in place? Who are you holding in place?

Decision Making – who says?

'For lack of guidance a nation falls, but many advisers make victory sure' (Proverbs 11:14)

I was leading the Prayer and Praise meeting in the Parish Hall and it was just not lifting off. As a result I was singing just a little bit more loudly and enthusiastically than I should have been in order to boost the meeting. As I looked heavenward to the Lord for guidance as to what I should do next the Lord said to me, 'Take a step back'. I was already aware that my contribution was from the flesh rather than from the Spirit, so I literally and physically took a step back from the microphone. But I did more than that. I took two steps back and said in response to the Lord, 'It's all yours'. Immediately the reply came, 'I have called you to lead'. So I took one step forward again. If someone in the congregation had their eyes open at this point they must have thought that I was doing the Cha Cha Cha and preparing to audition for *Strictly*!

The Bible has got a high view of leadership both in the Old Testament and in the New. Leaders are a gift from God. He appointed them for the security, guidance and encouragement of his people. Patriarchs, judges, prophets and kings in ancient times and then apostles, prophets, teachers, elders and overseers in the new church which Jesus founded. This has been the pattern of God's provision for his people over the millennia. Leaders are meant to lead. It is that short sentence which has focused my decision making over the years. For better or for worse the Lord has called me to a role of leadership and the implication of that is that I must lead.

In Aberystwyth our decision-making structure was as slim as it could possibly be. Our 'Wardens' Meetings' were held over lunch once a month. It included the serving clergy (Rector and Associate Vicar), the two church wardens and our church administrator. Like every committee meeting and every staff meeting it always began with item number one, 'Things that thrill the soul'. We would recount to each other the stories of things that were going well in the life of the church, and when relevant, in our own personal lives. That set the scene for the rest of the meeting. The agenda was open ended so that anything could be raised before we parted from each other. This was the executive arm of the decision-making process.

Peter Brierley of Brierley Consultancy draws on a census of 2002 in the Scottish Church. He writes that 'one of the findings was that the size of the team was important vis-à-vis church growth. Growing churches had an average lay leadership of thirteen people; churches stable over the previous eight years had an average team of nineteen people and declining churches a team of twenty-two people. The smaller the leadership team, the more effective it proved to be. A smaller number of people, willing to take risks, able to think ahead strategically and to identify the vision were better than a larger group with other wider gifts.'[1] It was heartening to find that this was a principle which we had already embraced.

In effect, the Wardens' meeting was the Standing Committee of the Church Committee which had fifteen members and was responsible for the overall decision making of the church. As a matter of policy we had no other sub-committees. Some might see that as a weakness, but I have to admit to having a deep suspicion of committees. George Barna, an American researcher in church leadership comments, 'Leadership by committee is an oxymoron.'[2] Too few church committees are committed to action. They are happy to write reports and make recommendations but are usually risk averse so don't actually do much. We need working parties or action groups rather than committees.

---

[1] Peter Brierley, *Coming up Trumps: Four Ways into the Future* (Carlisle: Authentic Media, 2004), p. 16.
[2] George Barna, *Turning Vision into Action: Defining and Putting into Practice the Unique Vision God has for your Ministry* (Grand Rapids, MI: Baker, 1996), p. 138.

Over the years I have observed some really underhand behaviour by clergy as they have tried to ensure that the church officials who are elected are the ones that they want. So in advance of the annual church meeting they will be ensuring that their chosen ones are nominated and seconded. They will seek out some of the influential people in the church and make sure that they speak up for the selected candidates and vote for them, so that when the election comes it is just a formality as all the work has been done secretly in advance.

Another terrible model for making appointments which many of us have witnessed is the 'pass the parcel' method. If a post still remains vacant on the church committee then there is an attempt made to apply leverage to various people who are present in the room at the AGM. 'You'd be good at this' is the comment made to someone who might possibly be persuadable. Then that's followed up by the 'minimise the commitment' method. 'It's not a demanding post and doesn't require a lot of time.' I always think that is such an insult both to the post which needs to be filled and to the person who is being invited to fill it. By the time that the person in the chair has finished they've made the task appear so unimportant that it sounds as though it isn't really worth doing. What a contrast to Bonhoeffer's comment that 'when Jesus calls a man, he bids him come and die.'[3] When we are inviting someone to take on a role in the life of the church, let's build the role up to being something that a person would want to commit their life and time to doing.

We wanted to ensure that we had the best people as church officers and members of our Church Committee, but we did not want to be underhanded or manipulative. As church leaders in St Michael's we made an unconstitutional decision which was implemented with the permission and approval of the annual general meeting each year.

---

[3] Quoted in David Watson, *Discipleship* (London: Hodder and Stoughton, 1981), p. 19.

It was already a by-law of the Church Committee that a person was elected for a three-year period whilst according to the constitution the wardens were allowed to be in post for six years. In order to be entirely transparent with the congregation we asked permission for the new appointments each year to be made by the leadership of the church rather than by election. So at the wardens' meeting names would be proposed and discussed and agreed upon. Those names would then be submitted to the Church Committee for their approval explaining the reason for the selection of each person.

Carl F. George, an American church growth consultant writes, 'A church that hands most of its ministry slots to elected positions is on a collision course. Elections too often operate on popularities, not ministry competencies.'[4] There were certain non-negotiable criteria for consideration in the appointment of people as wardens and Church Committee members. Obviously, first and foremost we wanted people 'filled with the Holy Spirit and wisdom'[5] who were fully committed to our vision to be in leadership and in positions of influence in our church. No minister would want anything less than that.

But we also wanted to avoid dynasties developing where people might think that they had a right to a particular position and that they could serve for thirty years without interruption, freezing out newcomers and other fresh ideas. We also asked that husbands and wives didn't serve together in order to avoid doubling the influence of any particular viewpoint (so my wife was never on the Church Committee).

We also wanted to maintain a broad spread of representation from the congregation so that we had both men and women from a varied age range, that we had people of a variety of backgrounds, and that we didn't just keep going round and round in a circle of the people

---

[4] Carl F. George, *How to Break Growth Barriers: Capturing Overlooked Opportunities for Church Growth* (Grand Rapids, MI: Baker, 1993), pp. 151-2.
[5] A basic requirement for deacons. See Acts 6:3.

who had been in the church for a long time. We wanted to keep our representation as broad as possible and to keep our Church Committee fresh. There was nobody better placed than the senior officials of the congregation to spot talent, to draw in a wide spread of membership, to ensure a good gender balance and to give as many people as possible the opportunity to serve on the committee.

This unconstitutional procedure could not have happened without the knowledge and agreement of the congregation year on year. It was not something which could have been implemented in my early years in St Michael's but was the fruit of longevity in post and also of providing trustworthy leadership overall. We explained every year the reasons why we operated the policy and as a consequence it was of immense benefit to the life of the church.

Continuing in ministry in a particular church for a period of twenty-five years would be viewed by some as a huge mistake. They might perhaps point to the fact that St Michael's peaked in its attendance some seven or eight years before I retired as an indication that I should have gone sooner. They would say that the statistics speak for themselves. In fact, statistics are only part of the story, and there is an on-going debate regarding how long a minister should stay in post.

Interestingly around the time of our peak attendance in St Michael's, I was having a three-day retreat at the Harnhill Centre of Christian Healing near Cirencester. The retreat was coming to an end in a communion service on the last morning. I didn't feel that I had heard anything new or special from the Lord and was wondering whether I had wasted my time, apart from the obvious benefit of having had a few days away from the parish. However, the speaker at that communion service drew on one significant illustration from his own experience. He described how he had reached something of a personal crisis in ministry after twelve years in the same post and was asking the Lord whether he had missed his guidance in some way. The Lord had said to him that if he had some other sphere of service for him then it would have been impossible for him to miss it. I didn't need to hear anything more. I had the re-assurance I had come for and found myself weeping in the arms of the speaker at the conclusion of the service as he prayed for me.

Research has shown that longer ministries are more fruitful than shorter ones. Longevity is not a guarantee of growth, but short ministries appear to be a guarantee of a lack of growth. In the light of that research it is amazing that some of our denominations are committed to a policy of shorter rather than longer licences for their clergy. Indications show that it takes between three and five years to change a church, but if the minister moves at that point the congregation will most likely go back to the way that they were before. If it takes between three and five years to bring change, it takes seven years to bring transformation. The difference between change and transformation is that the congregation won't want to go back to their old ways. Nothing could be more disheartening for a minister than to move churches and then hear that the congregation they have just left has undone all their hard work within months of their departure.

It will take up to five years to begin to feel fully bonded to a congregation. Within that time there will have been funerals, weddings and baptisms taking place, and those are the life events which bring minister and people together so that they have a common history. That kind of bonding cannot happen quickly. Experience indicates the immense value of serving over the long term. There is time to dig deeper in a teaching and preaching ministry. There is time to be patient with people and not to hurry them or hassle them into decisions. There is time to make deep inroads into the local community. There is time to see big projects through from their inception to completion. There is time to build enduring trust between the minister and the people and the fruit of that will be substantial.

There is of course one major challenge which has to be faced in staying in the same place for several decades, and that is the avoidance of stagnation. How does a minister stay fresh having already preached twenty Easter sermons and twenty Christmas sermons to the same congregation? That's down to a combination of the work of the Holy Spirit and what happens in the minister's study. We need to remain sensitive to the whisper of the Spirit. We need to maintain our prayer life. We need to study carefully and consistently. We need to be listening to what is going on in the world around us. We need to be open to the voice of God in and through the congregation. It is our interaction with the people we serve during the week which will often dictate the direction we take and inform our teaching and preaching.

So am I saying that I was never tempted to look elsewhere during that twenty-five years? I did have one invitation to apply for a parish in England, but that conversation didn't last for very long. We had been called to work in Wales and that call had always been crystal clear. It would have been inconceivable that having spent so much time and effort in learning Welsh that I could have ever considered serving in a parish where Welsh was not a requirement for the post. That effectively cut out speculating about other parishes in the cities of South Wales as well. Any move would have had to include a substantial proportion of ministry in the Welsh language. The reality is that the Lord didn't call us anywhere else anyway so moving or attempting to move would have been disobedience.

One of the big blessings of that period of ministry was the relative stability of our circumstances. There were fairly frequent changes of personnel because of the size of our ordained and lay team, and we did have one additional church (Llanychaearn) added to the original four which formed the Rectorial Benefice, but we did not have to face the upheaval that more recent re-organisations within the diocese have produced.

'Before the Spirit came no one wanted to lead', said Bertie Lewis to me about St Michael's Aberystwyth, 'but after the Spirit came everyone wanted to lead.' How human is that? Everyone wants a share in the glory. Or do they? Moses wanted the Lord to send someone else to lead the Children of Israel out of slavery in Egypt.[6] He was on the cusp of greatness. Everyone would remember his name for all time, but maybe he had caught a glimpse of the cost involved in leadership. He was certainly very reluctant to take on the task that the Lord had prepared for him. Perhaps it is true that reluctant leaders are the best ones because they are not in it for their own glory.

On one occasion I stood in the hallway of our home and said to the Lord, 'I don't mind dying. I just don't want it to hurt so much.' Leadership is painful. Paul said, 'I die every day.'[7] What he meant was that he was dying to what he wanted, he was dying to himself, he was dying to his ambitions, he was dying to his reputation. The church grows by means of the death of its pastor. Leadership comes at a price and no leader has yet been born who has been able to avoid paying it.

There are some Christians who do not like to talk about leadership. They feel that it is all to do with domination and that the gospel message challenges that idea. The gospel preaches equality, they say, which of course is true. 'There is neither Jew nor Greek, slave nor free, male nor female; you are all one in Christ Jesus.'[8] Within the family of God there should be no racial, social or gender inequality. This truth was lived out by Jesus through his example and is emphasised here once again in Paul's letters. Yet at the same time Paul was insistent that his apostolic credentials should be recognised and along with those credentials his apostolic authority too.

Not only did he insist on his own authority, but he ensured that in each of the churches for which he had responsibility there were elders appointed to supervise and lead the congregation. There were elders as well as apostles in the church in Jerusalem from an

---

[6] Exodus 4:13.
[7] 1 Corinthians 15:31.
[8] Galatians 3:28.

early stage,[9] and elders were appointed for leadership and were given authority wherever the gospel took root and new congregations were formed. Leaders were God's gift to the church then, and they are God's gift to the church now so long as they are godly and faithful.

Leadership was recognised by Paul as being one of the spiritual gifts which God gives to certain people. He spoke about it in his list of gifts recorded in his letter to the Romans, the one who has the gift of leadership, 'let him govern diligently.'[10] When he was writing this, Paul surely must have had in his mind the comment about Joshua from long ago who was described as 'a man in whom is the spirit of leadership.'[11] There is a gifting from the Spirit which brings an anointing on the life of a leader. It is that anointing which places the leader in a position of authority. The epistle to the Hebrews picks up on that theme and presses it home, 'Obey your leaders and submit to their authority. They keep watch over you as those who must give an account. Obey them so that their work will be a joy, not a burden.'[12]

When leadership is exercised in the way the Lord commands it will have the Spirit's anointing and be caring, protective and joyful. There is no hint of being controlling or dominating here. Rick Warren has an important distinction between domination and leadership. He says, 'I haven't known everything that happens in Saddleback for years. I don't need to know about it all! You might ask, 'Then how do you control it?' My answer is: 'I don't. It's not my job to control the church. It's my job to lead it.'[13]

---

[9] Acts 11:30, 15:2.
[10] Romans 12:8.
[11] Numbers 27:18.
[12] Hebrews 13:17.
[13] Quoted in C. Peter Wagner, *Churchquake! How the New Apostolic Reformation is Shaking up the Church as we know it* (Ventura, CA: Regal Books, 1999), p. 90.

Some other Christians have suggested that the whole idea of leadership is unspiritual. They would argue that this is a secular emphasis and one which should be avoided in the church. But we are not interested in the imitation of secular principles for we belong to a different realm. Our emphasis is leadership through service which was Jesus' attitude. 'I am among you as one who serves'[14] was his great statement about leadership. If we want to become great leaders, then we must first of all become great servants. Those who jockey for position and want to be first are the very ones who are disqualified from any kind of leadership influence in the eyes of Jesus.

When I was in conversation with the late Bishop Stephen Neil and bemoaning the lack of training for leadership I had received at theological college, his reply was, 'You don't need to be trained to be a leader. You need to become a man of God.' That was a pretty strong statement and a very short conversation!

So how do we hold these two ideas in tension, that on the one hand godly leadership is from the position of a servant, whilst at the same time Jesus appointed apostles to carry forward the work of the gospel and they in turn appointed elders to take responsible decisions regarding the direction and vision of the church? There is in fact no conflict between these two ideas. The leader is to lead but does it from a position of servanthood and submission to the leading of the Lord.

King Abijah of Judah was the one who got it absolutely right. He was in a position of national leadership. He called the shots, he made the decisions, he set the strategy for the nation, he carried forward the vision, but he said 'God is with us; he is our leader.[15] This was a theocratic kingdom under a human ruler. Leadership is exercised in submission to the supreme headship of the Lord himself. It is a leadership which has an ear open to the Lord expecting direction, correction and affirmation. Any leader who

[14] Mark 10:45.
[15] 2 Chronicles 13:2.

thinks that they can be independent of the principles already laid down by the Lord, or independent of the guidance of the Spirit is destined to make some awful and costly mistakes.

If King Abijah had got his vision right, it was Moses who got his strategy right. As he was thinking through how he was going to lead the Children of Israel he looked at them and said, 'You are too heavy a burden for me to carry alone.'[16] The result was that the people were given the opportunity to choose for themselves the leaders that they would like set over them to take them to the promised land. This was an entirely pragmatic decision but one which was necessary for Moses' mental health, let alone for the benefit of the people themselves. The outcome of the policy was that the people had the leadership that they needed even if they didn't always listen to it or respond as they should.

Delegation is the only way in which a minister will survive in a growing church and the only way in which the gifts of the congregation will be released in all of their fullness. There are some churches where the gifts of many of the individual members are completely wasted as they sit in the congregation week by week and find themselves de-skilled by an omni-competent minister. Instead of the minister flourishing and every member of the congregation flourishing there is a diminution in the life of the church. It is a lose/lose situation for everyone.

D. L. Moody, the American evangelist wrote, 'I'd rather get ten men to do the job than to do the work of ten men.'[17] We can wear ourselves out by trying to keep a tight rein on all the decision making and all of the activity going on in the church but the end result of that is exhaustion, breakdown and a severe limitation on what can happen. Church growth specialists tell us that one minister working alone can cope with a membership of a hundred.

---

[16] Deuteronomy 1:9.
[17] *Living quotations for Christians*, edited by Sherwood Eliot Wirt and Krirsten Beckstrom (New York: Harper & Row, 1974), p. 142.

After that any new people who are added in the top, result in an equivalent number of people falling out of the bottom.

Right from the very beginning of the formation of a luncheon club for the elderly I told the two volunteer couples who were taking on the initiative that they were in charge and that as it was going to happen regularly on a Thursday - my day off - they would never see me present. The Mature Munch, as it came to be called, has flourished for over thirty years. There are people in heaven today because of that ministry, and there are others who have been cared for and loved and supported and encouraged, and all without the presence of the minister. I would attend their Christmas dinner because that was so good, and accept one speaking engagement each year, but apart from that I had nothing to do with it, other than to enjoy the good news of over fifty people sitting down to an excellent lunch followed by a clear Christian message.

Similarly, another initiative which came from St Michael's in the year 2000 was aimed at providing employment during a serious downturn in our national economy. We formed St Michael's Services which eventually employed three men and together they had the capacity to do small building jobs around the homes of our church members and wider community. It would have been impossible for me to organise and supervise such an enterprise because I had neither the time nor the expertise for such work. However, our Church Manager at the time had all of the necessary skills and as a result it was an initiative which flourished for a number of years.

This principle of delegation came into its own when I was asked to become Area Dean of Llanbadarn Fawr and because of the number of clerical vacancies I was to become immediately responsible for twenty congregations. Five of our own and fifteen new ones. It quickly became clear that organising a spread sheet of weekly services for all of these churches together with people to lead them was going to be an absolute nightmare. It would require an enormous amount of time ringing retired clergy and lay readers and worship leaders to see who would be available when. In addition to that, there would be the paperwork to organise, the occasional services of funerals, weddings and baptisms to cover, and then the urgent pastoral work when people were hospitalised or bereaved. How on earth could we take that on in addition to everything else? That load alone without what I was already doing would lead to breakdown.

In order to solve the problem, we called a meeting of all the retired clergy, lay readers and worship leaders living in the area and explained the issue to them. My solution was to ask each one whether they would be kind enough to take on just one of the congregations for a period of time, perhaps for twelve months to start with, whilst we waited for the diocese to find new clergy to come to the area. One person looking after just one congregation and doing so with a light touch might be sufficient to solve the problems facing us. That way the church could have a service at the same time each week with the same person taking it. That has always seemed to be the ideal to me, and still does.

What I was not prepared for was the way that meeting was going to turn out. Everyone present was willing to be involved, but instead of each one taking on a single congregation they formed themselves into teams and took over all of the churches, appointing one of their number to be team leader. I walked away from the meeting that evening with nothing left to do except to take the praise for the decision which they had made!

'Trust, but verify'[18] was President Ronald Reagan's motto when he was dealing with the Russians during the Cold War. It is not that there is a war going on between leaders and led, but there is a need for someone to ask the hard questions, and to face up to reality when things are not going well. When we delegate, we don't dump responsibility onto someone and then walk away. We all need constant encouragement over the long term and when we don't

---

[18] A Russian proverb taught to Ronald Reagan by Suzanne Massie an American scholar. See https://en.wikipedia.org/wiki/Trust,_but_verify.

verify it is easy for people to become slack, to settle for less than the best, and to excuse or justify decline. In order to keep our leaders accountable, we would invite them to come to our Wardens' lunch from time to time in order to report on their ministry and to check on their progress. We wanted to verify their progress.

One of the greatest weaknesses I have observed among some leaders is their lack of willingness to repent when they have taken a wrong turn or made a bad call. We, as leaders should be at the forefront of those who repent before our congregations when we have got things wrong. Whether it is in leadership decisions associated with the life of the church which have been destructive rather than constructive, whether it is in some comment or teaching which we have given from the pulpit which was clearly wrong, whether it has been some maladministration on our part, we should be quick to repent and ask the forgiveness of our congregations. They should hear the voice of their minister expressing sorrow, apologising and asking for forgiveness when the blame has been theirs. It does the church no good at all when the leader 'hunkers down' and seeks to ride out the storm over some misjudgement on their part. We are all so good at blame casting and at blaming our advisors or blaming our congregations for our mistakes. It always leads to an unhealthy spiritual atmosphere and a rapidly declining attendance. People will simply go elsewhere, or not at all, having lost faith in the integrity of their minister.

'Please forgive me' is a moving appeal when it is made by the minister to the congregation, but not of course when the leader is using that as their *modus operandi* for continuing to live in a sinful and undisciplined way. However, used as necessary, it can be a superb way to model repentance and forgiveness in a church context. There were a number of occasions when I had to ask that the recording of a particular sermon was removed from the database of the church and not published on the web. The congregation would be told on the following Sunday that there were aspects of the sermon which were wrong or mis-judged.

What the leader is, the church becomes. The leader is as fallen as the congregation and it does the people good, and it does the leader good too, to be reminded of that from time to time.

'Everything rises or falls on leadership'[19] writes John Maxwell, an American leadership expert. He may be over-stating his point a little, but not much. Leadership is absolutely key to the local church and to the national church. We need to give our leadership skills more attention, not less.

Thinking moment

- Leaders must lead: does your congregation and church committee give your leaders enough room to lead effectively?

- 'Everything rises or falls on leadership'. Is that true, or is it overstating the case?

---

[19] John C. Maxwell, *21 Indispensable Qualities of a Leader: Becoming the Person others will want to follow* (Nashville, TN: Thomas Nelson 1999), p. xi.

Resolving conflict

'If you have been trapped by what you said go and humble yourself; press your plea with your neighbour' (Proverbs 6:2-3)

One of the things that most people would never believe is how rude some church members think they can be, and are, towards the clergy and their families. A colleague recently commented, 'You didn't tell me that when I got ordained that would mean that I would have a target drawn on my clerical collar.' He too had begun to experience what most ministers learn within months of being ordained which is that some people can be unbelievably offensive towards the clergy.

One of the questions on the blood donor questionnaire has always made me smile. 'Do you have a hazardous occupation?' For someone in Christian ministry there is only one answer to that – absolutely, yes. Quite obviously the minister is a 'representative of God' so if a person has got an issue with God, and they can't lay their hands on him, then they'll have a go at the next best thing which is more often than not their minister.

Whether they think that they are on safe ground because the clergy will not retaliate, or that the minister should be able to take some straight talking or that a 'servant of God' will always be forgiving, I cannot say. All I know is that on many occasions some people have said the most insulting things and behaved in the most unkind ways. Although I'm dealing with resolving conflict in this chapter please also believe me that we have seen the most startling generosity, the most humbling compassion and the most loving care extended towards us.

It took me longer than it should for me to learn that the resolution of conflict begins with me forgiving, long in advance of any face to face conversation which may or may not be necessary. In the early stages of retirement, I was asked during an interview what I thought was the biggest lesson that any minister had to learn. My immediate response which required no reflection was 'learning to forgive.' At one time I used to think that the Christian attitude towards the unkindness and criticism from others was to develop a thick skin so that they could say what they liked but I would be entirely protected inside my armour. Such an attitude was mistaken and worse than that, underneath it was a lie. I didn't have a thick skin. My skin didn't get thicker the longer I was in the ministry. I was hurt just as much as anyone would be by some of the things that were said to me. To pretend to people that they could say what they wanted and that I wouldn't mind was untrue. I did mind and I still do.

With every new offensive comment, with every new personal attack and with every new act of opposition the burden and the pain grew heavier and heavier. There is a low growing plant called Rest-harrow which is common on arable land. It has a lovely pink flower like the pea, but there's a special reason for the name of the plant. When the horse pulled the harrow across the field in the olden days, sometimes it would have to stop as the implement became clogged with the roots and tendrils of the plant. It would become too heavy for the horse to manage. That so closely describes the experience of the minister who has not learned to forgive. Their ministry will be clogged and either slowed down immensely or brought to a stop. As I look back now, I cannot believe how long it took me to realise that there was only one way out of the disappointment and pain. It was to forgive, frequently, daily, and in detail, the small offences as well as the large ones.

'Christian forgiveness is not leniency', writes Swiss physician and author, Paul Tournier.[1] We don't let the other person off the hook by forgiving them, and the hard conversation may still lie ahead. But we let ourselves off the hook because un-forgiveness does so much damage to us. If we think that what was done or said to us was bad, then we need to consider what allowing bitterness to take root within us will do. It will be far worse for us. It'll keep the

---

[1] Paul Tournier, *Escape from Loneliness* (London: SCM Press, 1962), p. 151.

hurt alive inside. We've all met people who are vengeful and resentful decades on from the original offence. Kate Fordham writing about the breakdown of her marriage says, 'Forgiveness is not nearly so much of a full-time job as resentment.'[2] The reality is that forgiveness is the one power that we always have over anybody who hurts us. Unforgiveness is torture, not to the person who has caused the offence but to the one who has been hurt. Unforgiveness simply perpetuates the pain, always. There is no end to it.

In the famous wineries of France and Spain we see huge vats containing gallons and gallons of wine. On a wine tasting tour, maybe our guide will draw off a taster from a vat or two allowing us to have a sip of the different vintages. Supposing in a moment of neglect the guide left the tap open, the tour finished, the lights were turned out and everyone went home. The vat wouldn't be emptied in an instant because there would be so much wine inside, but if the tap was left open, probably by the next morning, the entire vat would be empty and all the wine would have drained away. When we leave the tap of forgiveness wide open, then that allows the offence, the hurt and the pain to drain away over time.

In 1660 Parliament passed an Act of Oblivion which was a general pardon for all who had committed crimes during the English Civil War. What a fabulous concept. An act of oblivion passed on the offences that have been committed against us so that we deliberately don't bring them to mind any more, and neither do we recount the story of them to others. 'Forgiveness is not just an occasional act; it is a permanent attitude,' said Dr Martin Luther King.[3] This is the attitude which a pastor must adopt if they are going to be effective over a lifetime of ministry.

---

[2] Kate Fordham, *No Pit too Deep: Diary of a Divorce* (London: Lion Books, 1982), p. 76.
[3] *The papers of Martin Luther King junior: Vol VI, Advocate of the social gospel: September 1948-March 1963*. Clayborne Carson et al, eds. Berkley, CA: University of California Press, 2007. Sermon notes,

For many of us who do not like conflict (and I count myself amongst them) we may be reluctant or unwilling to have any kind of personal confrontation. But we do not forgive someone so that we can avoid difficult conversations. We forgive them so that the difficult conversation can be conducted with much less emotion and far more objectivity. Forgiveness is not an excuse to back down and back out of difficult circumstances. Nonetheless, the purpose of any one to one meeting is not to score points but always to achieve reconciliation and understanding.

Wonderfully Jesus had already anticipated that such occasions would be necessary and he has given us detailed instructions how to deal with them.[4] The first step is to deal with the matter one to one and with no-one else present. The point at issue is not to win the argument but to win the person. If it is a private matter between the two of us, then it should not be necessary to involve anyone else in what is about to happen. The matter should be kept confidential. We find this so hard to do because we often want to recruit opinion to our side before the conversation begins to be sure that we have a support group which thinks as we do.

One of the more difficult aspects of confidentiality is that if the matter is very serious then not only will we be praying about the meeting, but we will also want others to help to carry the weight of intercession. This is more easily shared when we have a supportive spouse, but we also may need the insights and prayers of trusted confidants.

As the years have passed there have been a number of areas of progress for me over these difficult one to one meetings. I have arrived better prepared with my thoughts down on paper and a list of issues that I want to discuss. In addition, I have learned to be

Draft version; Sermon preached on 03 April 1960 at Ebenezer Baptist Church, Atlanta, GA.

---

[4] Matthew 18:15-17.

direct in my language. Sometimes because of our reluctance or embarrassment we can be so oblique in what we are saying that we are not fully understood, or assumptions are made in filling in the blanks which are quite incorrect. Frankness and transparency can actually be of benefit to both sides so that there is no misunderstanding of the issues involved and of the feelings which have been hurt.

Jacob is instructive in his preparations before meeting his estranged brother, Esau. Not only did he pray extensively through the night, but he also put aside a substantial gift for his brother as a demonstration of the fact that he wanted there to be peace between them and for their relationship to have a future.[5] On this occasion the offending party was Jacob himself who had been at fault, but the principle of taking a bunch of flowers or a box of chocolates or an exotic pudding with us to a one to one meeting establishes from the outset that our intention is the continuation of the relationship and a commitment to reconciliation.

In my experience it has rarely been necessary to go to level two in Jesus' instructions. He says that if we're unsuccessful on our first visit then we are to ask someone else to come with us to establish the seriousness of the matter and to reinforce the particular view which is being expressed. Only on two occasions where the matter under review had legal implications did I ever feel it was necessary to bring in someone else.

In certain circumstances these meetings to resolve conflict may not bring about a meeting of minds on contested aspects of theology or church practice. But then the point of the meeting is to create an atmosphere in which differences can be recognised and acknowledged. To learn to disagree agreeably is a great achievement in the church and one which brings honour to the Lord.

---

[5] Genesis 32:13-20.

These principles are effective when we have been the offended party, but they also work when we have offended others. There are occasions when the minister has said something, has made a decision, has implemented a policy, has inadvertently upset someone in the congregation, and that 'offence', whatever it is, needs to be dealt with immediately, without delay.

The longer an offence remains, the more it has time to fester and to get worse. A phone call or an email is an inadequate way of dealing with such issues. We need to be able to look one another in the eye. We need to repeat the apology, if one is necessary, until it has been accepted and resolved. I have asked people to please forgive me, occasionally with tears. And I have been unwilling to leave their company until I have heard them say the words themselves, 'I forgive you.' I don't just want to ask them to forgive me, I want to hear them say that they have taken that step and have forgiven me. From that point on if they rescind their forgiveness or they said it but didn't mean it or if they continue to engage in a low-level condemnation of me then that becomes a matter for them. That is between them and the Lord. I have dealt with the matter to the extent that forgiveness has been requested and verbally given. It will obviously take time for the wound to heal and for trust and friendship to be restored and we will have to work at that and be prepared for it.

It's always helpful if this kind of meeting happens on their territory where they feel safe, in other words in their home if they are prepared for it. Sometimes if the discussion needs to be lengthy then a meal together at our expense may be appropriate so that there is plenty of time available for the resolution of issues.

None of us likes conflict (or shouldn't anyway) and none of us courts it, but when it happens we must be prepared to resolve it as quickly as possible and make that into the priority of the day. It becomes the top item on our agenda. Virtually everything else needs to be put to one side until the matter is resolved. Unattended conflict causes damage and it's vital that the minister takes rapid steps to resolve it.

One of the most outstanding characteristics of St Michael's Aberystwyth during my time there was the willingness to resolve conflict and to live together as a very diverse congregation. We had a congregation which included Reformed evangelicals and Roman Catholics, together with Pentecostals and members of the Salvation Army as well as other Nonconformists. There were High Anglicans and Low Anglicans; some who enjoyed ritual and some who wanted none at all and yet all of them were able to find a home amongst us because we were committed primarily to Jesus Christ and to being his disciples in practice not in theory. We gathered around him as our Lord and around the Bible as the authoritative source book for our faith.

In some larger towns it would probably have been possible for some of the members of our congregation to find a church which precisely ticked all the boxes of their theological outlook but in Aberystwyth the pool of churches to choose from is substantially smaller. Nonetheless, under God we were able to maintain a church culture which was both evangelical in theology and Charismatic in practice, but embracing enough to allow Christians from many different backgrounds to be entirely comfortable as they participated in worship and listened to the teaching.

United in the primacy of the Scriptures we were able to live together with a shared doctrinal outlook. We never experienced any theological controversy which divided the congregation. However, very often it is not matters of Biblical interpretation which cause conflict but aesthetics like music, audibility, furnishings, carpets and wall colours. Because these are such individual matters of personal taste, they can sometimes be more difficult to resolve than theological differences.

The development of trust between the leadership and the congregation is absolutely key to resolving these kind of conflicts when they arise. If the church members can see over time that their leaders are behaving responsibly and have good judgement, then they'll be willing to trust them decision by decision. This simply reinforces a point already made that longevity in ministry in the same place adds significantly to the authority which a leader can exercise over the long term.

We worked hard at keeping the congregation in the loop concerning decisions which were being made by the Church Committee. A précis of our committee minutes was published in the weekly bulletin on the Sunday following every meeting. We wanted to live as openly as possible in front of everyone and avoid the horrors of 'mushroom management' where everyone is kept in the dark for as long as possible on all issues under discussion. To this end, particularly in my early years in St Michael's, we would produce 'green papers' which were literally printed on green paper and were an outline of matters which were under consideration. These were consultation documents and church members were invited to make their responses and any representations to the wardens or to members of the committee.

We had two non-negotiable principles to guide us. One is that we aimed to make God honouring decisions by a God honouring process. The other is that we remembered that people matter more than things. 'I have become all things to all people so that by all possible means I might save some'[6] wrote Paul.

Thinking moment

- How good are you at forgiving? How good are you at apologising and asking for forgiveness? Have you any issues outstanding that still need to be dealt with? Have you witnessed an act of forgiveness which has impressed you and given you a model for the future?

---

[6] 1 Corinthians 9:22.

- Do you think that there are some issues which are so serious that it is unreasonable to expect the injured party to forgive? Doesn't forgiveness allow the guilty person to get away with what they've done? Surely forgiveness is not just.

Out of the pulpit

'Every word of God is flawless' (Proverbs 30.5).

I have always had a high view of preaching. Since that day in Hele Road Baptist Church in Torquay when the preacher made such an impact on my soul at the age of twelve, I have thought that preaching was important. Since then I have seen the effect of Spirit-inspired preaching for myself with entire congregations moved to repentance or moved to rejoicing and thrilling praise. I have felt the atmosphere at the conclusion of a sermon when the Spirit has been at work and the people are in awe of the Lord with long queues of people down the central aisle waiting for ministry and prayer.

Preaching is still honoured by the Lord and used by him for the benefit of his church. God has a high view of preaching; after all, he only has one Son and he made him a preacher. That Son of his was the most gifted preacher the world has ever seen with a life changing message, superb down to earth illustrations and applied with unerring accuracy.

As Anglicans we believe in Word and Sacrament. This is a fundamental commitment of our denomination, that we should preach the Bible and administer the sacraments. In Aberystwyth we were committed to the preaching and explanation of the Bible wherever and whenever there was an opportunity. So there was always a brief address at the 8 am communion service every Sunday. There was another one in the middle of the week on a Wednesday morning. No service would take place without a sermon. That was an invariable principle. It included infant baptisms on a Sunday afternoon, it also included wedding ceremonies and funerals. All of those sermons would be prepared afresh (apart from the baptismal service for which I had an evangelistic address which I had learned by heart).

To miss the opportunity to explain what Christian marriage looks like when we have a church full of people, or to fail to explain the Christian expectation of life beyond the grave when we have a large congregation of mourners in front of us, seems like a serious dereliction of ministerial responsibility to me. Very often our funerals will be attended by many hundreds of people who have not been inside a church building since the last funeral they attended. We must speak to them of the Christian hope of resurrection and invite them to consider their position before God. Similarly, at Christmas time when we have our largest attendance of the year, the wonderful readings from the Bible which are inspired and powerful need explaining and applying to people who don't understand what they are hearing. Just like the Ethiopian from long ago in his chariot who was reading the words of the Bible, but he needed someone to tell him what they meant.[1]

I cannot accept the argument from colleagues who say that the sacraments of baptism or communion speak for themselves and don't need any explanation. The sacraments don't speak for themselves. They need to be explained and made relevant. Sometimes it is horrifying to discover how little some people know of their faith although they have attended worship for their entire lives. For others who may come to a communion service as their first experience of church, they will find themselves in a world they do not understand. At a certain point in the service everyone else will get up and go to the front and kneel down. What are they to do? Whilst the communion proclaims the cross and is therefore the most evangelistic of services, it also creates more embarrassment and a greater sense of exclusion of the new person in a way that nothing else can do. Even if the visitor is invited to come to the communion rail to receive a blessing that still says 'You are different from us. We understand what we are doing, and you do not. We're more in than you are.'

People will most certainly listen for longer than seven minutes if they are given something interesting to hear. They have no

---

[1] Acts 8:34-35.

problem watching a film which lasts for an hour and a half or more. It's an insult to those who have come to a service hungry to be fed from the Bible to only speak for ten minutes. We should not be apologising for preaching nor think that it has outlived its usefulness. The only one who wants us to think that is the devil. The preacher who begins with the comment, 'I will not keep you long' or 'You won't want to listen to me' has already lost the battle for the attention of the congregation. That preacher has done a serious dis-service to the ministry of the church too. We have a message to preach which has come from God himself. We must 'command' the attention of our congregations, not apologise for speaking to them. We have a message concerning the wellbeing of their immortal souls. What could be of greater importance than that? To apologise as we begin, undermines the significance of everything that we are going to say.

Nothing contributed more to my own spiritual growth and development over the years than the preparation for preaching week by week. No preacher can turn up on a Sunday and preach without first ensuring that their soul is right with the Lord, so that requires adequate inward preparation. It means regular and detailed confession. It means the continuing pursuit of holiness. Anything that would hinder the work of the Spirit, anything that could be pointed to as a hypocritical statement or viewpoint has to be dealt with in advance. I can feel the pricking of the Spirit in my conscience even as I write these words, and so I should.

If it wasn't resolved before climbing the pulpit steps, then the 'accuser' would quickly point out the inconsistencies to the conscience in the middle of the sermon. The sermon must first of all search the heart of the preacher before it searches the heart of the congregation. The resulting maturity in the life of the preacher is not incidental, but it is a thrilling by-product of the study and prayer that goes into weekly preparation.

What happens in the pulpit flows from what happens during the week, most particularly from what happens in the preacher's private devotions and daily Bible reading. There is no need to be dry on the Sunday when for the six previous days there has been such richness enjoyed in the Scriptures. In fact, the problem is not the shortage of material but rather its abundance and how it is to be cut down to fit the time available. What has excited our soul during the week will certainly excite the souls of our listeners on Sundays. If it doesn't excite my soul in the first place, then it's best not preached at all.

There is never any reason for us to be stale either, so long as we have the Bible open daily and so long as we are maintaining a reading discipline associated with our Christian discipleship. It has been said that, 'If a preacher will keep studying he will be better at fifty than at forty, and he will be better at sixty than he was at fifty', and may I add, better at seventy than he was at sixty.

Not only must we continue to read extensively but we must learn to guard our reading. It has taken me a long time to realise that the number of hours available to read is limited and that I must choose my material carefully. In parish life the clergy are constantly being told by members of their congregation that they have found this or that book to be helpful and the temptation is to try to read them all. The reality is that we need to be selective, that we need to learn to speed read so that more superficial books can be skimmed and returned quickly, but also that we need to risk offending people by saying, 'I'm sorry but I have got a long list of other books on the go at the moment and I won't be able to devote any time to this additional one.'

We were advised at theological college not to lose the benefit of our study but to maintain a filing system which allowed us to recover material from the books that we were reading. Mine is far from infallible (isn't a filing system a method of losing things alphabetically?), but it has been of immense benefit over the years and I cannot commend it too highly to those who are making a start in preaching. However, the greatest record of my studying over the years is actually to be found in my sermons. If material did not find its way into a sermon, then it was neither memorable nor sufficiently valuable to receive comment. We were advised to file our sermons according to Biblical text, but in addition to that I have a cross reference exercise book which records not only the text but also the title, date and place of preaching.

There are a variety of approaches to sermon preparation which I have heard commended over the years, from the preachers who spend every morning throughout the week working on their Sunday sermons, to those who read the readings for the following Sunday on a Monday morning and then allow the themes to 'stew' in the soul during the rest of the week. Each of us has to work out a system which works for us. I found that most of my sermon preparation was done on a Saturday. If I had started on a Monday morning, I could guarantee to still be working on it on Saturday afternoon as my preparation would have expanded to fill the time that was given to it. I'm the kind of person who needs the adrenalin of the last minute to get things onto paper. There were some occasions when that last minute began again at 5 am on Sunday morning if the Saturday had been unproductive, but that shouldn't really be admitted! I'm hopeless after 10 pm so there was never any point in staying up to burn the midnight oil. Let each preacher know themselves. I was heartened to learn that Charles H. Spurgeon, the Victorian Baptist preacher, would sometimes prepare his Sunday evening sermon on Sunday afternoon. A terrible example, but it worked for him. Those who preach expository sermons through a book of the Bible are delivered from the tyranny of having to 'find' a text at the last moment because next week's sermon is already given.

In the early days of preaching I would only have two sides of A5 for my notes, but as the years have passed those notes have become longer and longer. Now I know that eight sides of A5 will last 20-25 minutes and ten sides will be a full half hour. On the rare occasions that I have tried to preach without notes (a practice I really cannot recommend) I have found that I've strayed, been repetitive, taken a long time over illustrations, been far less pointed, followed every hare as it has emerged from the thicket and been generally dissatisfied with my efforts.

A young ordinand who was being trained for the ministry at Burgess Hall in Lampeter was given the task of preaching one Sunday evening in the local parish church. The vicar at the time asked the young man in the vestry before the service, 'Have you got your notes?' to which the student replied by tapping his temple and saying 'It's all up here.' In fact, at the end of the sermon the vicar was very impressed by this fluent young preacher and invited him back a second time some months later, only for him to preach exactly the same sermon again. Preaching 'off the cuff' will only work for those who have superb memories and are carefully prepared in their study in advance. For the rest of us it results in going around and around over favourite themes, hobby horses and stories until both preacher and congregation are tired of them. If we are going to preach for years and even for decades in front of the same people then we need constant freshness of themes, of idioms, of illustrations and of application.

To ensure that freshness in St Michael's we did a circuit of themes taking a book of the Old Testament, followed by a book from the New Testament, followed by a series on theological or ethical or contemporary issues, and then back to the Old Testament again. Our commitment was to Bible teaching with exposition and application at its heart.

The practice of starting a sermon with a joke is all well and good except that there are a limited number of acceptable jokes which can be used for such a purpose. Certainly not 52 of them a year, or 104 of them, if we're preaching two different sermons on the same day. Nonetheless we need to find bridges into the lives and experience of the people who are in front of us. We have breathed the same air during the week, have lived with our families although in different combinations, been to work although in different careers, have watched TV, heard the same news, share similar concerns and anxieties. We need to establish at the outset that we live in the real world, the same world that they inhabit and build bridges into the week that we've just experienced together.

We have only got a couple of minutes to capture and then keep the attention of our congregation. On one occasion I was in the congregation in a different church and was sitting behind a couple who had brought their child for its baptism which had taken place during the main service. After the ceremony was over the service continued and then the vicar went to the pulpit to preach. To begin with the mother of the baby gave her undivided attention to the preacher but after a couple of minutes she looked away and never looked back at the preacher again for the rest of the sermon. Her attention had been lost and the opportunity was squandered.

From a captivating introduction we then need to do a number of circuits with our material, making point number one from the passage in front of us. John Jones, Talsarn, in *Some of the Great Preachers of Wales* advises a new young preacher of the need to have 'six or seven bombs in every sermon, and after you have them take them with you into the pulpit. Then begin quietly and calmly and pave the way slowly and gradually for the firing of your first shell.'[2] These 'bombs' will already have exploded in the soul of the preacher. If they haven't then it's best not to use them. They need to captivate me first and if they don't do that then there's no chance at all that they'll have any effect on anyone else. I need to be preaching out of a warm heart which has been touched and inspired by the truths I'm about to share. We should feel often that we want to run to the pulpit because we have such a thrilling theme to share with our people. We should be on tiptoe with what is burning in our souls.

Then must come an illustration to illuminate the point, which is then in turn followed by an application of this truth to our lives. Point, illustration, application. 'Where application is lacking

---

[2] Owen Jones, *Some of the Great Preachers of Wales* (Stoke-on-Trent: Tentmaker Publications, 1997), p. 494.

something less than preaching occurs',[3] writes Dr Jim Packer. We may need to do this cycle several times in the same sermon to reinforce a particular idea or outcome.

Personally, I think in pictures, not in ideas. According to Aristotle, 'The soul never thinks without an image.'[4] All I can say is that I'm not a philosopher in any way. But, for my encouragement, it seems that that was the way that Jesus thought too, or if he didn't think like that then he most certainly preached like that. Taking a picture and describing it makes it live in the mind of our hearers. I'm aware that there are preachers who think in ideas and theological concepts and they really do have their work cut out to find and to accumulate pictures, illustrations and stories which will connect with their congregation. It's essential that they do this if they want to keep the attention of their hearers. 'He is the best speaker' says the Arab proverb 'who can turn the ear into an eye.'

It took me some time to become sufficiently ruthless in my preparation that I would leave out material that did not serve the overall purpose of the sermon or of the text in front of me. Sometimes we can be so wedded to working in a particular quotation or illustration that doesn't quite fit, but it's too good to leave out. It needs to be left out!

Creating a title for the sermon as the exposition of the passage proceeds during preparation in the study can be a very valuable practice. Not only does it focus the mind, but it also produces the brackets which should surround the material that is included. Those brackets will dictate what is included but they will also dictate what material is excluded too. The Scriptures must shape the title of the sermon, not the title shape the sermon (unless we're preaching on a particular theme), otherwise we'll be pressing the Bible to serve our theme rather than expounding what is in the text itself. However, the title can work as an abbreviated aim for the

---

[3] Quoted in Leland Ryken, *J. I. Packer: An Evangelical Life* (Grand Rapids, MI: Crossway, 2015), p. 369.
[4] *De Anima* (III 7, 431a, 14-17).

sermon identifying what impact it is intended to make. 'Will it do?' asked the young curate when he showed the draft of his sermon to his vicar. 'Will it do what?' came the reply. Good question.

There is nothing more lovely than for the preacher to be surprised by the teaching that emerges from the Scriptural text. The more that happens the better. It's reassuring for the congregation to hear from the preacher if they've discovered something new in preparation or reconnected with a known truth which has come with fresh and increased impact. It makes the listener feel less intimidated by their own ignorance which is a major problem for many congregations. So often I feel that when we invite people to come to a home group to 'study the Bible' together their main reason for refusing is not a lack of interest but rather a fear that their own ignorance will be exposed and paraded in front of others.

It is not a sin to be interesting. We must grab the attention and then hold it. We are in a battle against distractions, tiredness, and for some a simple unwillingness to listen. We must captivate the mind using every method available to us, keep our vocabulary uncomplicated and every day, and be accessible in the themes that we are presenting. Charles H. Spurgeon said that Jesus had told Peter to feed his sheep, not feed his giraffes.[5]

Reference to the original Greek is not usually very riveting for a congregation and is unlikely to be the subject of conversation at the dinner table later in the day unless it is one of those superb illustrations which makes the sermon stand up like a child's 3D picture book. A *huperetes* of Christ, is a servant of Christ,[6] but a *huperetes* is an under rower on a trireme galley. Imagine the man pulling on the oar to the beat of a drum and keeping in time with all of the others; imagine a servant of Christ sweating in his service to the Lord keeping in time with the beat of the Spirit. That's a 3D image, but these illustrations have to be used so very sparingly

---

[5] From his sermon, 'Feed my sheep', no. 3211 published on 18th August 1910.
[6] 1 Corinthians 4:1.

otherwise the eyes of our congregation will glaze over and they will enter another world which is not the world of the preacher.

It's been said that if you look at a Picasso painting for too long then you'll end up with both your eyes on the same side of your face. But Picasso said of his work, 'A good picture, any picture has to be bristling with razor blades.'[7] His work most certainly was. It was constantly challenging the art world of his generation and also challenging the people who stood and looked at his work. Similarly, Jesus' teaching was bristling with razor blades. He challenged the religious outlook of his era by exposing the hypocrisy of many and his disciples continued to do the same in their turn. When the people heard the preaching of the apostles on the Day of Pentecost they were 'cut to the heart.'[8] John Stott in his book *I Believe in Preaching* quotes Spurgeon's illustration of the knife thrower at the circus. There is a woman standing with her back to a large board and the knife thrower stands at a distance and plunges knives into the board all around the silhouette of her body. He aims to miss.[9] We preachers cannot afford to do the same. Our preaching needs to contain challenge as it confronts wrong thinking, tackles sluggishness and coldness of heart and deals pointedly with matters of the soul.

Even before we begin, the preacher needs to have in mind where the sermon is leading and what kind of response is appropriate. On most occasions the sermon will finish simply with a prayer re-emphasising the application of the material for the day and seeking the Lord's help and inspiration to put it into practice. But on other occasions something else may be more fitting. Perhaps for members of the congregation to stand in response to a call to repentance. Perhaps a sung response of the chorus 'He's my Lord' or some other hymn. Perhaps silence for a period to decide how to be reconciled with someone who has offended us. Perhaps

---

[7] Quotation on a wall display in the Picasso Museum in Malaga.
[8] Acts 2:37.
[9] John Stott, *I Believe in Preaching* (London: Hodder Christian Books, 1982), p. 251.

repetition of a pre-prepared prayer. Perhaps an invitation to come for prayer by the ministry team. Whatever happens it must not be the same as last week and the week before. Otherwise the response becomes yet one more ritual in the life of the church and the more frequently it happens the more it becomes robbed of significance.

In response to evangelistic preaching we have used multiple different methods to draw in the net of commitment. From inviting people to say a prayer under their breath and then ask for a copy of the prayer at the door, to standing in their place as a public indication of commitment to Christ, to coming to the front and kneeling in an act of submission to his lordship, to coming forward and signing on the dotted line a statement of commitment to the Lord, to coming to the front of church and standing on cut out footprints as an indication of a determination to be a disciple, to crossing the line of faith where we had taped a white line at the front end of all three aisles in the church and inviting people to come and physically step over it.

I am more and more drawn to the use of a decision card of some kind where people are given time to assess whether or not they are going to give their lives to Christ. Sometimes it has taken months before they have been ready to sign their names but when it does happen then it is very serious and much more permanent than a single momentary response.

I have kept my sermon notes from all of my years of preaching, not in order to use them again, but rather for reference regarding the material gleaned from my studies that those sermons contained. In fact, rarely have I preached the same sermon twice, apart from taking it to several churches on the same Sunday. It seems to me that if we are preaching a 'living' word then it has to live in each context when we preach. Though the themes may be the same, the proclamation will be different every time because the context will be different on each occasion.

Whilst I have devoted a substantial amount of time to dealing with the subject of preaching there have been two related factors which have not been mentioned. One of them is the place of prayer and the other is the activity of the Holy Spirit.

Prayer ought to be a given both for the preacher and for the congregation. We get what we pray for. There will be the daily devotional prayer life of the preacher and added to that the prayer life of the congregation. In St Michael's the Sunday ministry would be a constant theme in the weekly confidential 'Intercessor' prayer letter. It would feature regularly in the prayer meeting on a Friday night when the texts and themes for Sunday would be prayed over.

As to the Holy Spirit, it was said of John Wesley that at one time his preaching was like the firing of an arrow, all the speed and force depended on the strength of his arm in bending the bow. This was before he was under the influence of the Holy Spirit. Subsequently it was like the power of a pistol ball, the force depending upon the gun powder, needing only a squeeze of the trigger to set it off. I was an early product of the Charismatic Movement of the late 1960s. I had had my own encounter with the Spirit whilst out running one evening on the lane down to St David's Station in Exeter. The Spirit came in power on me that evening and I began to speak in tongues. That same Spirit has never been withdrawn and I'm conscious of my need to continually rely upon him. 'Apart from me you can do nothing'[10] said Jesus when commanding us to 'remain' in him. I continually remind myself of the dependence which is necessary upon the power of God and not the power of human eloquence or gifting.

'Help him Jesus', is the whispered prayer that any preacher needs to hear coming from the congregation. That's when the fire really begins to burn.

---

[10] John 15:5.

Thinking moment

- Do you have a high view of preaching? Should we really be listening out for the voice of the Lord when we listen to the preacher? Doesn't that exalt preaching rather more than we ought?

- What are the chief responsibilities of the preacher week by week, and what are the chief responsibilities of the listeners?

Self care

'Above all else, guard your heart, for everything you do flows from it' (Proverbs 4:23).

1. The Lord. 2. Spouse. 3. Children. 4. Ministry. 5. Self. That's the Biblical order of priorities. Any fiddling with that order, any attempt to change them around will lead to discord and breakdown. Life for the minister lived in this way will have a far greater chance of success over the long haul.

The first commandment is that we should love the Lord our God with all our heart, soul, mind and strength.[1] He takes first place. There are those who object to the proposal that the Lord takes first place over all. They would argue that this has been the problem in so many vicarages and manses. The minister has been too busy with the Lord's work to give proper emotional support to the family. But the reply to such an accusation is that the Lord's work is fourth in the list. First in the list is the Lord himself. There is an important distinction between the Lord and his work. They have different positions in our order of priorities. Anyone who has put the Lord's work before their spouse and children has committed a serious sin against them and against the Lord whom they serve. They will have suffered as a result of it and so will their family.

By contrast, putting the Lord first is no threat to our spouse or to our family. As soon as we go to the Lord and place him first, he turns around to us immediately and says that we are to take care of our spouse. 'Husbands ought to love their wives as their own bodies. He who loves his wife loves himself.'[2] This works the other way around too for wives to love their husbands. Who could ask for anything better than that? When the spouses are in love then the atmosphere in the home (and in the church) is all the sweeter. No-one can minister effectively when there is tension in

---

[1] Deuteronomy 6:5.
[2] Ephesians 5:28.

the home, and it won't be long before the congregation senses it. Then instead of the leader serving the church, the church starts to minister to the leader. That puts a stop to all spiritual progress in the life of the congregation until matters are resolved.

The need for spouses to pray together is immense. We have no problem being physically intimate with our spouse. We must lay aside any kind of embarrassment in being spiritually intimate too. My wife and I have prayed together almost every day for more than half a century. Praying together aloud is perfectly natural to us and it is that which has carried us through the stresses and strains of marriage and of ministry. This is the time when we are real with each other and with the Lord.

When the children see their parents in love and when they burst in to the bedroom to find their parents in prayer, then it is guaranteed that the children will feel secure and they'll have learned some of the great lessons of marital life from the example of their parents. They will have seen with their own eyes what it means to have a personal prayer life and what it means to call on the Lord for guidance, strength and comfort.

In order to guard our marriage, we would take every Thursday off together. The church knew that it was our day off. We would not attend meetings or organise events which required our presence on that day. Consequently, everything tended to slow down in the life of the parish. The undertakers knew that I would not be available for funerals apart from exceptional circumstances. That was a day for us. Some couples organise a weekly date night. We organised a weekly date day. Even in retirement we still try to keep Thursday as a day for us. Others laugh when I apologise that I can't do something on a Thursday and they say, 'but you're retired.' Yes, I am, and this is still our day. The protection of our relationship is more important that anything else.

Taking a Thursday off means that Saturday becomes a working day just like Sunday, so when do the children get a look in? Our answer was threefold. Firstly, I was present almost without fail at breakfast and our evening meal. The meal table was family time and if the phone went then it was either switched to answer phone or it was not answered. That way I would see the children at both ends of the day. Secondly, whilst Thursday was taken completely away from work there was still space in the evenings and on occasional Saturdays when there was plenty of opportunity for quality family time. Thirdly, holiday time was so memorable because of the adventurous and exciting things that we did together. They are now part of family legend and new memories are being created with the next generation of grandchildren.

In the order of priorities our ministry comes after our commitment to the Lord, to our spouse and to our children. Our spouse and our children need to know that and have it constantly reinforced in their minds that they are more important than our work. They too need uninterrupted space where they are given time and attention. Too frequently ministers convey the impression to their children that their needs are second to the needs of others in the church. That's very damaging for their emotional health and for their self esteem.

It has long been a word of caution to ministers that we are to love the Lord of the ministry rather than the ministry of the Lord. The problem for many of us is that the ministry of the Lord is so fulfilling and satisfying that we are reluctant to take time away from it. For some they begin to feel that the success of the work depends entirely upon them and that if they are not attending to their ministry constantly then it will start to fail. It is so easy for us to become co-dependent and for us to thrive by being needed by others who seek our counsel and advice. There are lazy clergy, but overall the besetting sin of ministers is over activity not under activity.

Last in the order of priorities are the needs of the minister themselves. Some would be reluctant to put themselves onto the list at all. They would see their inclusion as an act of selfishness.

'He must increase and I must decrease',[3] they would say. But too often breakdown comes in the life of a minister because it has been forgotten that they are human. We need to recognise our humanity and make allowances for it. Peter Brain writes, 'Most ministers don't burn out because they are ministers. They burn out because they forget they are people.'[4]

Right at the beginning of time the Lord was aware that human beings would need rest; at least one full day in seven. He set the example himself in the work of creation when he rested on the seventh day.[5] This then became a creation ordinance. It has been built into the fabric of our lives by the Lord himself. He included instruction concerning a day of rest in his ten commandments and put it at number four ahead of murdering, committing adultery and stealing. He reinforced the message with his people when he refused to provide manna for them on the Sabbath in the wilderness when they were travelling from Egypt to the promised land.[6] The manna from the sixth day kept until the seventh day, but only on that one occasion during the week. Every other day it rotted if they tried to keep it overnight. Then to emphasise his commitment to the Sabbath still more clearly, God the Father would not raise his Son from the grave on the Sabbath. Jesus had to stay in the grave from Friday sunset until Sunday dawn before the Father would raise him.

The fourth commandment to 'remember the Sabbath day by keeping it holy'[7] is the most widely broken of the ten commandments amongst Christian people today. If it was suggested to the average Christian that they were regularly breaking the commandments they would be incensed, and yet Sabbath observance of one day in the week when we do no work is

---

[3] John 3:30 (AV).
[4] Peter Brain, *Going the Distance: How to Stay Fit for a Lifetime of Ministry* (Youngtown, OH: Matthias Media, 2004), p. 256.
[5] Genesis 2:2-3.
[6] Exodus 16:21-30.
[7] Exodus 20:8.

widely ignored in the church. It needs to be restored to its rightful place for the spiritual, mental, physical and emotional wellbeing of us all. Ministers should take the lead in setting the example, rather than thinking that we have some kind of exemption. We should get our rest one day in seven. 'Remember', writes Carl F. George, 'your faithfulness or unfaithfulness as a pastor is not measured in terms of fatigue.'[8]

Not only do we need regular weekly rest days, but we also need those periods of time where we can take extended time away with the Lord. There are seasons when big decisions have to be made. There are seasons too of exhaustion even when we have been taking a regular day off. We get so depleted by the constant demands upon us and the needs of so many people that we have to attend to. Those seasons of retreat are especially important. It is better if they are planned, but if not, then we need to be ruthless in recognising when they need to be taken and that we are so run down that a retreat style break has become essential.

When we were in Aberaeron back in the 1980s one of our wardens said to us, 'You need to go away for our sakes.' He was absolutely right. If we are ministering out of exhaustion everyone can see it and the whole congregation suffers. We need to listen to our spouses over this too as they will be the first to observe the short-temperedness and the irritability. My wife told me on one occasion that I needed to go away and I was insistent that I was fine. Off I went to make yet another phone call and as I checked with the Lord on my way to the phone to see what he had to say the response was immediate, 'I want you there.' So that afternoon I packed and went.

When I got to the retreat centre, I asked the Lord what I was supposed to do and the reply was, 'Read Ezekiel' so I spent the subsequent hours reading through the book. I sat bolt upright when

---

[8] Carl F. George, *How to Break Growth Barriers: Capturing Overlooked Opportunities for Church Growth* (Grand Rapids, MI: Baker Books, 1993), p. 169.

I got to the sentence: 'Son of man look with your eyes and hear with your ears and pay attention to everything that I am going to show you, for that is why you have been brought here.'[9] What Ezekiel is then shown is a restored temple, the Lord returning in glory to his temple and then a blessing flowing from the temple firstly as a trickle, then a stream and then a river which is so deep and wide that it is too hazardous to cross. That prophetic vision has held me for more than three decades and was more than fulfilled during our time in Aberystwyth. Very often the river of people and the river of need was too deep to cross, but so too was the river of blessing.

There was a regular communion service at that retreat centre taken by a retired priest. He was a High Churchman, so he was wearing full vestments. Clearly he also liked incense so when it came to censing the altar the little chapel was filled with smoke. That's not a natural environment for me and I felt as though I was something of a spectator rather than a participant until suddenly it seemed as though I was standing before the throne of God, and a voice said to me 'What have you got to say for yourself?' I felt as though everyone in heaven was waiting for me to answer and I couldn't think of anything to say. Yet as I stood there, the Lord on his throne leant forward and without saying anything simply put his arms around me and embraced me. I returned from that period of retreat fully refreshed and even tempered again.

Like most clergy we have always found the Christmas period to be the most intense of all during the year. The demands of church work increase hugely as December goes by, yet there is no doubt that the Christmas events provide for us the greatest evangelistic opportunity of the year with carol services taking place from early in the month right through to Christmas day. In addition to all of the activities in church there are also the demands from the community, from the schools, the hospital and of course our own families and friends. We would find ourselves totally depleted at the beginning of every year so decided to take a short break in the

---

[9] Ezekiel 40:4.

sun on a regular basis in early January. On one occasion in what we thought was complete anonymity we ended up in a hotel in Tunisia only to discover that the people to whose table we were assigned were first language Welsh speakers from Cardiff and were familiar with our church and ministry.

The husband of our new-found friends had a high-powered job in Welsh cultural affairs. As we spoke about our exhaustion after Christmas, he echoed our experience but added that he now took three holiday breaks every year from his work and that he ensured that when he returned from one break he would already have the next one arranged. So he was working on the next but one break all of the time. 'That means' he said, 'I can work with intensity in the intervening period knowing that my next break is already arranged.' What wisdom. Having the next break on the not-too-distant horizon has been really important to us now for several decades. It doesn't have to be expensive or exotic, just away! It has given us something to anticipate when the demands have been extreme.

Jesus took his disciples away for rest. He invited people to come to him for rest. Those of us with an activist temperament need to learn the lessons of rest for the sake of our longevity in ministry. Those of us who have been raised on the maxim that it is better to wear out than to rust out, need to be reminded that it is better to do neither! It is best of all to still be 'in ministry' right up to the end.

For some ministers the sudden and complete stop that some holidays provide is not psychologically healthy for them. One of the solutions we have discovered, which worked for us (me!) is to have a 'holiday with a purpose' which is on offer through chaplaincies and locums across Europe. Whilst the children were young, we participated in the camp site chaplaincies along the west coast of France, and when they closed, we became involved in the permanent chaplaincies in Switzerland and Ibiza operated by the Intercontinental Church Society (ICS). These worked as a wonderful halfway house, avoiding the sense of 'idleness' which some people might enjoy and still gave a feeling of purpose and direction to the holiday period.

The apostle Paul is very specific that our bodies are the temples of the Holy Spirit. He was referring primarily to the need to ensure that we keep them sexually pure. But he concludes his argument with this statement, 'You are not your own; you were bought at a price. Therefore, honour God with your body.' [10]

If we are going to honour God with our bodies that means we will ensure that we give them the right amount of exercise and that we feed them with healthy foods. The danger for many ministers is that their lifestyle is largely sedentary. They are sitting at their desks, then they are sitting in meetings, then they are sitting with people and much of what they do is accompanied with food. Unless they build an exercise rhythm into their week, as the years pass they will find that they have lost ground where their physical health is concerned. This is an important matter. We should be ruthless about setting time aside to get proper physical exercise. We should be setting an example to the flock about our responsibilities to our own bodies because we want to be in the Lord's service for the long haul.

When I was a boy each teacher in school seemed to have a different suggestion for their pupils as to what they should do with their time whilst waiting for the bus in the morning. 'You could go over your French vocabulary', said one. 'You could do some mathematical equations in your mind', suggested another. 'You could think your way through a science experiment', said yet another. In the end we youngsters just chatted with each other on our way to school and forgot about everything else. We've all heard the advice flowing from 'successful' churches. 'You must have a date night with your spouse.' 'You should give at least one evening in the week to volunteering in church.' 'You need to spend an evening of quality time with your children.' 'You should spend more time with non-church people to make relationships with them.' 'You should give

---

[10] 1 Corinthians 6:19-20.

more time to serving in the community.' How many evenings do these preachers have in their week? I only have seven. It is God first always, but then priority of priorities is the family and then ourselves. We mustn't leave ourselves out of the picture. Jesus doesn't. 'Come to me all you who are weary and heavy laden and I will give you rest.'[11] That invitation applies to the minister as much as to the congregation.

The work of the ministry is not a job, it is a vocation. Yet it is more than a vocation, it is a lifestyle. We don't live over the shop, we live in the shop, for the flow of people in and out of the house is constant, and our office/study is in our home. For that very reason and to ensure that we can give a lifetime to this ministry we need to ensure proper protection for our spouse, our children, and ourselves.

Thinking moment

- Solomon says that we are to guard our hearts. What steps are you taking to guard yours? What steps are you taking to guard your marriage and the parenting of your children?

- A serious issue for many people today is sleep deprivation and being over busy. What steps should we take to protect the Lord's day and to use it properly and well ourselves?

---

[11] Matthew 11:28.

Into retirement

'For though the righteous fall seven times, they rise again' (Proverbs 24:16).

It would be easy to dismiss the growth of St Michael's Aberystwyth as an aberration because of the unique circumstances of the town. It is thronged with university students during term time and then filled with tourists in the summer. That would inevitably boost the life of the churches in any town. It is absolutely true that did happen.

Where the students were concerned, they were youthful, exuberant, and filled with life and creativity. It was such a pleasure to have them as part of our congregation. They kept us all young and on the back of their presence we were able to be more experimental than we otherwise could have been, and we were able to harness and use their gifts as well as their considerable energy and vitality.

It's also true that there were a large number of tourists who visited the town and the west coast of Wales. Many of them would treat St Michael's as 'their home church away.' We would see them year after year and hugely valued their support, appreciation and encouragement. They would often recommend us to their friends as well. However, if growth is down to location and social demographics then all other towns similar to Aberystwyth should have large Anglican churches at the heart of them and that simply isn't true.

There were five principles which combined to make the difference in St Michael's and we have seen them working equally effectively in retirement in a small rural setting on the coast of Cardigan Bay just five miles north of Aberystwyth. We retired to Borth in 2013 to maintain our close contact with the sea. For the first twelve months we enjoyed being part of a congregation with no responsibilities, but then our vicar moved parishes and we entered an extended interregnum. As a recently retired minister I was asked to help out and to cover the three churches in the group.

Interceding in prayer
During our time in Aberystwyth we knew that we were being prayed for on a regular basis by the members of our congregation. The Sunday ministry as well as the leadership of the church was being prayed about daily by many people. After going into retirement quite naturally the focus of prayers in St Michael's passed to my successor and he was the subject of those same prayers. Initially, it didn't matter so much because we were not very deeply involved in the life of the church in Borth, but if we were going to take up regular ministry again even though it might be for a comparatively short time we were going to need the prayer cover of people who cared about us. There was no doubt that if we stepped forward again into some kind of consistent weekly ministry, we would encounter a severe spiritual battle once more, and that has proved to be true.

We wrote to a number of friends asking them if they would become confidential prayer partners with us. We would send them a monthly update on progress and if there were problems then we would ask them to intercede for us. In the end we had a list of thirty-six names. All that we wanted was their prayers. As we had experienced before there was an instant atmospheric change as soon as that prayer support was put in place. It is impossible to explain but something was immediately different. It wasn't just that psychologically we knew that we were being supported but rather something changed 'in the heavenlies.' We were being picked up by people who pray.

In the light of our experience in Aberystwyth and our subsequent experience in the little parish of Borth, I would never start or engage in any kind of ministry without knowing that I had that kind of prayer backing. We seem to think that prayer is a kind of optional extra that the super-spiritual want to engage in. The reality is that it is absolutely fundamental to any kind of change or spiritual progress in any church setting. This is the door of influence that the Lord himself has given to us and he promises that he will reward openly those who pray in secret.[1] We will see the impact. There will be an atmospheric change.

Preaching the Bible
At that Church Growth International Congress in Seoul, South Korea all of those years ago I clearly remember Pastor Yonggi Cho describing the beginning of his ministry. He told us how he had attempted to be very deep and erudite and intellectual in order to attract the university academics and city professionals, and he described how it had been an utter failure as a policy. He went on to say that when he started to preach simply about Jesus thousands upon thousands of people came including the academics and the professionals. People want to hear about Jesus, and they want to be taught the Bible. When the Bible is preached in a clear, accessible and relevant way people will come.

Giving room to the Holy Spirit
One of our church members who is in her seventies said that she had never before heard anything about the Holy Spirit in all of her years of church going. How can that possibly be true, or acceptable? What neglect there must have been in the content of the sermons of so many who preached to her, over the years.

'Did you receive the Holy Spirit when you believed?', Paul asked the men in Ephesus. They replied, 'No, we have not even heard that there is a Holy Spirit.'[2] Where were they then on the day that John the Baptist preached on the coming of the Spirit? The Spirit may be neglected sometimes in our contemporary churches, but John most certainly didn't omit speaking about him, and these men in Ephesus knew all about his teaching and his baptism from the time when they listened to him preach on the banks of the river Jordan. When he pointed to Jesus the Messiah, he added that he was the one who 'will baptise you with the Holy Spirit and with

---
[1] Matthew 6:6.
[2] Acts 19:2.

fire.'[3] Were these men not concentrating that day? Perhaps they had a short memory? Maybe the day that John the Baptist preached this these men had an urgent appointment in Jerusalem. Or perhaps whoever told them about John's message had left out this central part of his preaching. One way or another they missed it.

The Holy Spirit is the one who brings Jesus alive to us. He is the one who makes the spiritual realm real. He is the one who empowers us to be different. He is the one who makes us like Christ. He is the one who gives us new gifts which we can receive from no one else. We need the Holy Spirit. He is the one who renews the church and who brings growth. 'Are you so foolish?' asks Paul when writing to the Galatians, 'after beginning by means of the Spirit are you now trying to finish by means of the flesh?'[4]

A church ministering in the flesh is the one which puts on concerts and other attractions to fill the empty pews. It promotes itself as a cultural centre or a community centre. It convinces itself that if the building is thronged with people during the week that equates to success. Anyone can fill a building if we can find good enough musicians or well-known celebrities. Opening a nursery or setting up a drop-in centre or making the church into a concert venue is using the building, but it is not building the kingdom of God. We need to be making disciples and for that people need to be converted, filled with the Spirit and pointed towards a lifetime of following Christ.

How can we possibly miss the Holy Spirit? And yet we can and do. Ignatius of Latakia, Orthodox Metropolitan, wrote this reminder for the worldwide church:

> Without the Holy Spirit God is far away, Christ stays in the past, the Gospel is a dead letter, the church is simply an organisation, authority is a matter of domination, mission is a matter of propaganda, the liturgy is no more than evocation, Christian

---

[3] Matthew 3:11.
[4] Galatians 3:3.

living is a slave morality. But in the Holy Spirit the cosmos is resurrected and groans with the birth pangs of the kingdom, the risen Christ is there, the Gospel is the power of life, the church shows forth the life of the Trinity, authority is liberating service, mission is Pentecost, the liturgy is both memorial and anticipation and action is deified.[5]

Creating a community
We need to create a close, bonded and unified family. For this to happen home groups of some kind are essential. Over a period of four years we saw growth in all three of our small country churches. The congregation of St Matthew's Borth rose from single figures to fifty on some Sunday mornings. Similarly, the congregations in St Michael's Eglwysfach and Llangynfelyn, two other congregations for which we were responsible, also grew. From no home groups at all we established three with a total membership of over thirty from all three congregations. When they all came together for a mid-week celebration, we had forty-four people present. We repeated precisely the same kind of programme as the one used in St Michael's Aberystwyth. Some of the material we continued to write ourselves on themes like 'A faith that works in the twenty-first century', 'What Christians believe', 'Getting to grips with Jesus'. 'What the Bible teaches about....' Some of it was pre-packaged like the Bible Course and the Prayer Course. All of it was adapted to where our people were at that moment.

When we finished one course then we took a break. As we started the next course, we were able to go back again to those who hadn't joined us the first time around, and we kept on inviting people especially those who had shown an initial interest but may have been shy about coming. In this way the groups grew. At the beginning we started with one group in our own home, which is not a vicarage, but when we got to twenty-seven people it became unsustainable even though we divided up into different rooms for discussion. Often people need more than one invitation and

---

[5] From the address of Ignatios IV at World Council of Churches Assembly in Uppsala in 1968.

starting new courses after a break gives that opportunity to go back to people a second time, a third time and even more.

The thrilling thing that happened is that we saw prodigals coming home to the Father. Some after fifteen, twenty, twenty-five years and more. One returned prodigal has recently taken communion for the first time in thirty years during lockdown on her own in her home. There have been conversions too as people have come from a position of no faith to a living personal faith and are committed to grow in Christ. They must tell their own stories, but they are heart-warming and thrilling.

Prioritising Evangelism
My father died when I was just eighteen months old and my brother was five years old. Just before he died, he asked my mother to remain faithful to him and not to marry someone else. By this time, she was in her early thirties and was still an attractive woman. Despite now being a widow with children she would have had no difficulty in attracting admirers and possibly another husband. I would have been glad to have had a father figure and could never have blamed her if she had broken her promise to my father. In my view he should never have asked it of her in the first place, nor should she have agreed, but she considered faithfulness to her promise of greater importance than her own needs which were considerable. She now had to raise two boys as a single mother. My father's last words to her were honoured. How much more should we honour Jesus' last words to his church to go into all the world and proclaim the Gospel and to make disciples in all nations.[6]

In order to reach out to the community here we ensured that every home in the village received an invitation to our main festival services. So at harvest time, Christmas and Easter we printed a well designed flyer which was hand delivered through every letter box. We then put on some lovely community services and were once again reversing the downward spiral of the past four or five

[6] Matthew 28:19-20.

decades. Our Christmas services had record attendance with over 200 at our Carols by Candlelight with the church absolutely bulging - children sitting on the pulpit steps and the communion rail, and the choir stalls filled with people too. One of the men from the village had expressed doubts to me that we could ever fill the church again for a service, so publicly I asked the people present to take him the message, 'Told you so!' He heard that the building had been packed within half an hour of that service being over.

We introduced a Carnival Sunday service and called it 'Ice Cream Sunday' (not original to us). We introduced a couple of small children's activities into the carnival programme as well, to pick up from the Borth Beach Mission which used to run in the village some fifty years ago.

It was a refreshing challenge to be back in a rural community again and to watch the spiritual development of small country churches. We've seen how worship can change from being exclusively organ-led to the use of a viola creating some haunting and heart stopping moments. Static churches which had become used to having the same people turning up week by week were delighted to see new people coming through the doors as we prayed together, 'Thy kingdom come, and thy will be done in Borth, Glanwern and Ynyslas; in Taliesin, Tre'r-Ddôl, and Llangynfelyn; in Eglwysfach, Furnace and Glandyfi'. And his kingdom has been coming and his will has been done there.

So has it all been plain sailing again? Uninterrupted years of growth and evangelistic success? Of course not. The battle has continued and been unrelenting. That is the nature of ministry. The devil has been as busy as ever if not even busier and at times the opposition has come from some most unexpected and unwelcome sources. Jesus prophesied that those who are his disciples will face opposition. He forecast that some of it might come from within the family, and even possibly from within the family of faith.[7]

---

[7] Matthew 10:36.

Yet these five principles which worked so well for us in St Michael's Aberystwyth have worked for us again in these three small churches. The God of the one is the God of the others. These are timeless principles. Biblical principles. God's principles. Yes, in some ways the growth came more slowly, just as it tends to do in a rural setting. Yet although we were working in a more traditional context, nonetheless as these principles were implemented the growth came. 'The Lord has done this and it is marvellous in our eyes.'[8]

But hasn't the church moved on in the past eight years since retirement? Won't the church be unrecognisable once Covid 19 has passed and life returns to normal? That depends upon who you listen to and who you believe. There are some doomsayers who are prophesying that up to 25% of our church members will never return, whilst there are others who are celebrating the new people who have been contacted through online services and what they see is the 'growth' of a virtual church. Which way will the tree fall?

One thing is certain, the church of Jesus Christ will continue to thrive simply because it is his church. It is quite likely that some more of our denominational structures will collapse because of lack of finance, lack of personnel, lack of vision, lack of members and worst of all a loss of Biblical truth. Some are prophesying that only about ten years remain for the institutional churches. That may be so, but the encouragement is that there is still plenty of vigour, energy, vision and faith remaining amongst the people of God and they will carry the cause of Christ forward.

At the beginning of this book I began by extolling the virtues of Solomon the wise. He presided over the nation of Israel which during his reign, in terms of territory, was the largest that the world has seen to date. He wrote his impressive books on wisdom which repay serious study and the implementation of his principles. But, of course, in his later years he dropped the ball.

---

[8] Psalm 118:23 and Matthew 21:42.

We read that he had married strategically. By the time he had cemented alliances with the city states around him as well as the nations to the north and the south he had acquired 700 wives, and there were an additional 300 concubines as well. Strategic though many of these marriages may have been they were in complete defiance of a clear command of the Lord not to intermarry with the pagan peoples which surrounded Israel. 'They will surely turn your hearts after their gods',[9] the Lord had told his people.

Solomon is to be admired when we hear that 'he held fast to these women in love.' How praiseworthy that he should treat them with such respect and affection. But marrying in disobedience to the Lord, even though it was a 'politically correct' thing to do, and extremely wise, was in fact the thin end of the wedge. The thick end of the wedge which he most certainly could not have foreseen at the beginning was that he would eventually agree to the building of shrines to Ashtoreth, Chemosh and Molech, pagan gods of fertility, sexual licence and child sacrifice. To this day the southern hill of the Mount of Olives which overlooks Jerusalem is called the Hill of Scandal. It was there that Solomon himself worshipped these gods in plain sight of the temple to the God of Israel which he had built. How could it have come to this, that a man who had witnessed two personal appearances of the Lord, who had been blessed in such an outstanding way, who had written some books of enduring value, that he could end his days bowing in front of pagan idols? What a warning to any Christian leader.

Some of the people and ministries which I have quoted approvingly and admiringly in this book have come to tragedy either doctrinally or morally. I trust that the reader will be selective and wise enough to recognise the principles which should be imitated and those things which should be rejected. These leaders were not all wrong all the time. In fact, for many years their ministries prospered and were an immense blessing to the wider church.

---

[9] 1 Kings 11:2.

It is something of a mystery to us where exactly God draws the line between blessing and using his ministers, and the point at which he withdraws that favour and the church or the minister becomes Ichabod - 'the glory has departed.'[10] There are no perfect ministers. All of us carry our failings and weaknesses with us and regrettably those imperfections will infect and affect our ministry throughout our lives. Mercifully, the Lord has given us a way to effective service despite our failings, and that is through repeated and daily repentance together with repeated and daily forgiveness. Holiness has been described as falling 1000 times and getting up 1001 times.

Whilst we wanted it to be known that St Michael's Aberystwyth was committed to growth in numbers and spiritual maturity, we would also have wanted it to be known for the holiness of our character. At the end of the day what counts most of all is not how many people were attending the building, but rather how many disciples were living the life. That aspiration remains unfinished business for all of us. Holiness remains the pursuit of the serious disciple to the very last breath.

'If you think you're standing firm, be careful that you don't fall.'[11] That's the warning from the Apostle Paul. It isn't always in the area of our weaknesses that we fall, but sometimes in the places where we feel that we are strong and unassailable. 'It takes a steady hand to hold a full cup,' says the old proverb.

I must be as alert as Solomon should have been in order to finish well. One of the issues which caused me to hold back in my commitment to Christ when I was seventeen was the uncertainty that I could 'keep it up.' I had tried several times during my teens to finally nail my commitment to Christ but had pulled back because of the pressures of others around me. If I made that full and final commitment to Christ, could I keep it up? It was in the midst of that confusion of mind that I came to realise that at the end of the day if this was really of God, then he would by his grace

[10] 1 Samuel 4:21.
[11] 1 Corinthians 10:12.

keep it up in me. That's the way that it has been over the years and I trust that is the way that it will be until the finishing line whenever that may come.

Thinking moment

- Five principles surrounding prayer, teaching the Bible, the activity of the Holy Spirit, creating a community, and evangelism. Are they in the right order? Would you add anything to this list or remove anything from it?

- Are they in evidence in the life of your congregation? If they were, would you expect further growth to be taking place?

An accidental prophecy?

In 2004 I was interviewed by Llewellyn Jenkins for a book he was editing on contemporary Welsh preachers. He printed my responses to his questions verbatim and concluded the interviews in the following way:

> *How do you see the medium to long-term future of the church?*
> I think that in another thirty years the religious and spiritual landscape of Wales will have changed totally. There will be wholesale closure of churches and chapels right across the land, but a new church will rise up, a church quite different in kind from the one that exists at the moment.
>
> *A unified church? One church – a Church of Wales?*
> No, I don't think so, not particularly. You'll certainly see more action at a local level; more Christian groups getting together in village halls or in homes. In some senses the church of the future will be more primitive; I don't think that it will have glorious and expensive buildings. It will be smaller, very serious about its faith and explicit in its message. As a result, it will be much leaner and fitter than today's church. And I think it will have shed its denominational identities and its traditions and will have become much more of a pilgrim church; a church that is on the move and is going to accomplish something for Christ. I look forward to seeing that.
>
> *So there are real reasons for optimism?*
> Yes, because the Lord is not going to leave Himself without a witness in Wales.[1]

Only eighteen years have passed since that interview rather than the thirty I predicted. The rapidity and the extent of the change in the Christian landscape in Wales has taken me by surprise, particularly now that I am involved in planting a new congregation

---

[1] Llewellyn Jenkins (ed.), *Contemporary Welsh Preachers, Volume One: Where is faith?* (Harleston: Leaping Cat Press, 2004), pp. 72-3

in a village hall of all things; just as I had predicted for others. Five local Christian couples have come together to form a new fellowship and we are meeting in Rhydypennau Community Hall in Bow Street, north of Aberystwyth, just three miles from where we live.

At the end of July 2020 during lockdown a member of one of our village churches initiated a service on Borth beach in the open air. An invitation was sent out to all the known Christians in the area of every denomination. On the day everyone was appropriately socially distanced and there was a healthy sea breeze. All those attending, including myself, saw it as an interdenominational gathering of friends and not a formal act of Anglican worship and on that understanding I had accepted an invitation to give an address. We were inside the thirty-person limit for socialising but when informed about it after the event our diocesan authorities deemed that it was illegal under the guidelines of the Welsh government at the time. That conclusion is still contested by those who arranged the gathering.

However, that August I received a letter from the Bishop of St Davids withdrawing my Permission to Officiate in the diocese. I enquired as to the reason for the decision and received a reply from the bishop's PA saying that 'the granting of PTO (Permission to Officiate) is entirely in the gift of the bishop, and therefore no reason need be given regarding its withdrawal. If the bishop had wanted to share anything further with you regarding your PTO withdrawal she would certainly have done so in her letter to you.'[2]

Despite this decision being challenged by a substantial number of friends both locally and across the diocese, there has been no change regarding my position. However, it may well have been a blessing in disguise because on 6 September 2021 the Governing Body of the Church in Wales (effectively the church's parliament) voted to allow the blessing of the relationships of committed same-sex couples.

[2] Email received on 7 August 2020.

The withdrawal of my Permission to Officiate in the diocese was nothing more than a 'little local difficulty' in comparison to the enormity of the decision which the Governing Body had made. For decades there has been an on-going debate in the Anglican church world-wide regarding the Bible's teaching on homosexuality. For some the acceptability of same-sex sexual activity has been seen as a matter of love, acceptance, tolerance, compassion, equality and justice. They have declared this to be a 'second order' matter and not central to the church's teaching. The suggestion is that all may embrace this without compromising their Christian commitment.

The appeal of these arguments sounds very persuasive and to oppose them appears to be nothing more than bigotry and homophobia. However, the debate over homosexuality is masking a much deeper and, dare I say it, more important debate about the place of the Bible as the primary authority in the Christian church. For, if the Bible is mistaken in its teachings about homosexuality, then it may be mistaken over all that it teaches concerning sexual ethics. The Biblical teaching on same-sex sexual relationships is consistently negative towards them. On six separate occasions the Bible refers to the matter and uniformly declares it to be wrong.[3] Now, if the Bible is mistaken about homosexuality then perhaps it is also wrong about sex before marriage, about sex outside of marriage, about multiple partnerships, about polygamy, about polyandry, about incest, about prostitution, about pornography. If it is wrong about sexual ethics, then perhaps it is wrong about its other ethical teachings. And if it is wrong about ethics then maybe it is wrong about God and Christ and salvation and the after-life. Maybe it is just a relic from a four thousand year old desert religion from the Middle East after all and has no relevance for humanity today.

It is not an over-statement to say that the argument over homosexuality is actually an argument for the soul of the church

---

[3] A helpful overview of this debate can be found in Sam Allberry, *Is God anti-gay? And other questions about homosexuality, the Bible and same-sex attraction* (Epsom: The Good Book Company 2015).

and this is the reason why there has been such division amongst Anglicans around the world. Homosexuality is the presenting issue, but the authority of the Bible is the underlying issue. As a result of our differences over the place of the Bible in our church's teaching there is now a parallel Anglican church in North America and another one which is emerging here in the UK with the Anglican Convocation in Europe. This is not a rarefied debate for academics in theological colleges, but it has implications for every congregation across the country even as far as the small community of Rhydypennau in the west of Wales.

For many of us in the Church in Wales this has been a red-line issue. We are emphatically not anti-gay, but we are emphatically pro-Bible. Had I not already had my Permission to Officiate withdrawn then I fear that I would have had to return it to the diocese as this new provincial policy would have made it difficult for me to continue serving the church into which I had been ordained over fifty years ago.

In October 2021 just a month after the decision was made, we launched Fellowship 345. The preparation for it was already in the planning, but our direction of travel was confirmed for me by the Governing Body's decision. We deliberately decided to meet at 3.45 pm in order not to conflict with any other service taking place in the local area. Anyone who wished to come to us could still attend a morning or evening service in their own home church. We advertised it as an 'additional' service and not an 'alternative' service, and despite calls for us to meet in the morning we have consistently chosen to keep to the original timing.

Right from the very outset we were at pains to ensure that no-one could think of us as a single-issue congregation or say that our existence was purely based on our objection to the new position on sexual ethics adopted by the Church in Wales. We took two bases of faith as the foundation for our fellowship, both that of the Evangelical Alliance UK and also the Jerusalem Statement which came out of a meeting of orthodox global Anglican leaders in

Jerusalem in 2008. Although we have not yet formally joined the Anglican Convocation in Europe which is the fellowship of congregations, leaders and individuals who wish to continue to be Anglican, I have placed myself under the episcopal leadership of Bishop Andy Lines who co-ordinates the Convocation.

As a tease I was tempted to give the name of 'The Cave of Adullam' to our new fellowship. That was where David went to hide when he was being chased by Saul, the first king of Israel. The Biblical record shows that 'all those who were in distress, or in debt or were discontented gathered around him and he became their commander.'[4] When we remember those people who gathered at Adullam became the seed from which a united Israel grew, the title could be considered especially appropriate.

Over the years ministers have been warned about 'church hoppers', those who are never happy in whichever church they attend. They are continually on the move from one place to another trying to find the church which pleases them completely. We never expect them to stay, knowing that they will always be looking for the next congregation to join. However, there are two things to say in response to that very valid warning. The first is that many of us within the church have little idea of the offence and hurt that we have caused to so many people outside it. There are large numbers of people who have been deeply wounded by the church and by its failure to pastor them compassionately and consistently or show even the vaguest interest in them. Many have been upset and hurt by ministers and members of our congregations. The reputation of Christ has been tarnished in their view. We need to go to them repentantly and with sincere apologies in an attempt to win them back.

But, secondly, there are a substantial number of people who are now leaving the Church in Wales and who are doing so conscientiously. They are withdrawing not because they are offended, but because they are holding on to a Biblical stance

---

[4] 1 Samuel 22:2.

regarding faith and morality. These people are amongst the most faithful worshippers you could find in any church. They are conscientious about attendance, about commitment to discipleship, about sharing their faith with others, about generous and sacrificial giving. Currently, the church is not losing the stragglers, the half-hearted and the less committed, but they now have people who have been at the core of church life, wardens, treasurers, PCC members, administrators, pastoral visitors, readers, worship leaders and even clergy stepping away by choice and saying, 'I am conflicted about leaving, but I cannot remain here'.

Covid will have concealed the decisions of many of these people because some will have quietly slipped away saying very little as they do not want to hurt the feelings of those who remain behind. When church attendance is fully restored and all of our buildings are fully open once more, their places will remain empty. They will be amongst those who do not return. Some of these congregations will have been so depleted that their future will be very uncertain indeed and some will close in the not too distant future. Some of these people have already found their way to Fellowship 345 and to other similar churches which are being established. We naturally face the accusation that we are taking people from other churches, whilst the reality is that we are offering a spiritual home to those who have already decided to leave. The Anglican landscape of Wales is changing profoundly and rapidly.

However, I am rightly reminded that as there are those who conscientiously have chosen to leave the Church in Wales because a red line has been crossed, there are others who are equally conscientiously remaining within the denomination staying faithful to Christ whilst hoping that they can still do something about that red line and maybe rub it out at some time in the future. I admire their commitment and respect their decision and continue to pray lovingly and longingly for the same outcome, but now from the outside not the inside. Still Anglicans, but not part of the Church in Wales.

For all of my ministry, I have been disappointed when people have left our churches to join an independent congregation or go over to Nonconformity. I have done my very best to persuade them to stay. I have frequently used the lovely piece of advice which has been around for many decades that if you are part of a frozen church it's possible that the presence of your bottom may melt the ice, but if the ice starts to freeze your bottom then it's time to leave. All the evidence at the moment is that the ice has frozen our leaders and influencers, and for me now it is time to leave.

So, here we are once again building a congregation and approaching it with the same five practical principles in mind that this book is all about, principles which have 'worked' in the past in our experience and the experience of so many others over the centuries.

The priority of prayer; we are still drawing on the love and support of our prayer partners as well as meeting ourselves for a time of intercession on a Wednesday lunchtime. The preaching of the Bible remains our enduring theme. An openness to the Holy Spirit; very shortly we expect to be establishing a prayer ministry team and to develop still further the spiritual gifts of all of the members of our fellowship. The building of community; this needs immediate attention as we are a gathered congregation and not one with a geographical parish. An emphasis on evangelism; just a few months after starting we have the pleasure of our members bringing with them people who are not yet believers and others who have never been to church before.

We have every reason to expect that this work will grow as a result and that the Lord will add to our number those who are being saved.[5] 'A church on the move' is what I had forecast, 'and which is going to accomplish something for Christ'. Nothing less than that will satisfy us.

---

[5] Acts 2.47.

Thinking moment

- A time to stay and a time to leave. Which is it for you now? Are you freezing the block of ice, or is the block of ice freezing you?

- Five principles which apply to church growth have been outlined in this book. Which do you think are the most important? Are any of them lacking in the congregation where you are currently worshipping? What could you do to restore them to prominence?

Printed in Great Britain
by Amazon